Finding
HOPE
During Uncertainty

Finding
HOPE
During Uncertainty

Delena Stuart-Watson

Carpenter's Son Publishing

Finding HOPE During Uncertainty

© 2022 Delena Stuart-Watson

All rights reserved. No part of this book may be reproduced or transmitted in any form or by any means, electronic or mechanical, including photocopying, recording or by any information storage and retrieval system, without permission in writing from the copyright owner.

Published by Carpenter's Son Publishing, Franklin, Tennessee

Published in association with Larry Carpenter of
Christian Book Services, LLC
www.christianbookservices.com

Edited by OnFire Books

Copy Edited by Ann Tatlock

Interior Design by Suzanne Lawing

Printed in the United States of America

978-1-952025-94-5

To my father, who has been my role model my entire life. Through the years, I saw you be an example of what a godly man looks like. During the most difficult times of my life, I would look to you for guidance. I wish you could have read this book before God took you home. I am so proud of our family as we are striving to fulfill the legacy you left behind.

Daddy, I love you.

Table of Contents

Introduction

Life is a collection of moments, some planned, and others unexpected. In these moments we are growing, learning, and sometimes groaning, depending on which season we are in. Some seasons feel abundant, while others seem desolate with unexpected sorrows.

If you are reading these words, you may be hurting, for yourself or a friend, or for a child you love. We've all experienced pain at one point or another in life and no one will escape it. In *The Problem of Pain*, C.S. Lewis wrote, "Mental pain is less dramatic than physical pain, but it is more common and also more hard to bear."[1]

Whether you are surrounded by family and friends or in a quiet waiting room, when you go through pain you probably feel alone, forgotten, and helpless in making the pain go away. I have experienced tremendous pain in my journey here on earth and I wrote this book as a way to provide hope for others in their own storm.

Having a child who develops complications, medical issues, or physical issues puts you in a group no one would choose willingly, yet so many of us are here—questioning, hurting, and afraid to hope.

---

1. C. S. Lewis, *The Problem of Pain* (New York: Macmillion Publishing Co., Inc., 1962), 156.

I am a member of this group, a parent who knows first-hand what it's like to have a child who has unexpected medical issues. I understand what it's like to not be able to hold your baby, to not know if it's going to survive any given night.

No matter what is going on in the world around us, this child takes up every moment of your day and night as you wait on the doctor's call, administer medications, or perhaps wait for the moment you can touch your baby's hand.

Friends and loved ones who surround us with care do their best to be encouraging and helpful. They try to lift our spirits through clichéd words and advice that isn't very helpful at times because unless they've gone through a circumstance like this themselves, they will never fully understand how to help. It is like no other pain you can experience—to see your child hurting. Soon, if your child's medical issues are ongoing, your circle of support seems to dwindle away completely, leaving you feeling more alone than ever.

If you are in this group like I am and you are helplessly suffering alongside your child, know that you are not alone. This book was written for you. As you read the words of this book, you will come to understand we share many sobering commonalities.

Maybe you had your baby rushed out of the delivery room, as I did, leaving your arms empty. Maybe your baby's first home became the children's hospital, while the cradle at home remained empty. Infant bottles and toddler spoons may have been replaced by feeding tubes and various medical equipment. Maybe you spend your days and nights on the fold-out chairs in the hospital room, listening to your child's cries of pain, and you can't even hold them or rock them to sleep.

Once we get our child home from the hospital, as wonderful as that is, it doesn't mean the issues are over. Social engagements we used to take for granted become a rarity as we cancel many of them at the last minute due to a change in our child's condition or because of the financial strain we are experiencing.

We also know that on any given day, a routine doctor's visit can result in our child being rushed to the hospital and quickly admitted for an emergency surgery. Medical lingo is now our second language, and we wait, patiently, for updates and reports while our child spends countless hours in surgery. As parents in this group, we seem to have become more familiar with human anatomy than most medical students.

I have also experienced another hard reality as a member of this group. It seems the moment we try to get our head above water and connect with life outside the hospital, we're immediately faced with the bills that accompany our child's medical issues. I also understand what it does to a family when your or your spouse's employment is terminated for missing too much time at work.

Before long, money can get so tight that we are left searching the floorboard of our car for pennies, hoping to have enough to pay for hospital parking so we can go home to get a change of clothes. I know what it's like to be weighed down with so many medical bills that other necessary bills go unpaid and that dealing with debt collectors can become a hated regularity.

I think the hardest part, though, is the feeling of constant dread and the feeling of being utterly alone. Some even question the existence of God. I have been there, and I know where you are now. It's that unfamiliar place where the normal path of life no longer exists and you find yourself in need, being the receiver of support instead of being the one able to give.

Over the years, I have verbally shared my experiences with others who have found themselves unexpectedly in this group—a parent who has a child with medical issues. They communicated to me how helpful it was to find someone who knew their language, who truly understood what they were going through. This book is in response to their encouragement.

The following chapters will chronicle the birth of my daughter, Ragan, and our journey as mother and child to survive. My ultimate goal is to offer you a sense of peace and encouragement as you realize you are not alone no matter what situation you are in. At the end of each short chapter, I have included some reflective points for you to ponder that I have found helpful through the years, and even now, I find myself referencing them often.

During the writing of this book and now that it has been published, I continue to spend time in prayer for those who read these printed words. Although I don't know you personally, I know that God hears my prayers for you—the mother, the father, the family member, or the caregiver.

Delena

I can do all things through
Christ who strengthens me...
Philippians 4:13

Chapter 1

The Problem

Lack of Control

"Kirk, I need you to come home from work. My contractions are increasing."

Of all the days, my husband Kirk was at the golf course working late trying to complete inventory of the pro-shop. But when he heard concern through my voice, he raced home and agreed that this was the night we would more than likely be heading to the hospital.

"I thought the doctor said it wasn't time?"

"I know what the doctor said, but these contractions are becoming more intense and closer together."

Throughout the evening, I could not get comfortable, and Kirk kept asking if we should go to the hospital. I just kept reminding myself the doctor had said earlier in the day that it was not time, but I soon realized he was wrong.

With Kirk's livelihood rattling around in the back of the car, he drove his golf clubs and me to the hospital in record time as traffic was pretty light that time of night. We were greeted by a nurse who had been in contact with our doctor since we had called ahead, and she was given instructions to check us in, keep me monitored, and slow the contractions down until morning.

Now in the hospital room with hours to spare until the doctor's morning arrival, I had plenty of time to mull things over in my mind. Thankfully, I'm a planner. Even though it was still eight weeks until the baby's official due date, we were prepared. We had ooh'ed and ahh'ed over the baby shower gifts and were amazed at how generous everyone had been in helping us prepare for this new member of our family.

From precious onesies and necessary baby lotions to a handy stroller, we were blessed to be so well taken care of by our family and friends. I was there during so many of their children's births, and it was finally my turn! I knew this little bundle would change everything, and I couldn't wait!

I loved the baby's room. It was peaceful and just right, designed in pastel green with a touch of pink, blue, and yellow so that a little boy or girl would feel right at home. My mother-in-law and I had made all the bedding, and I had painted the baby bed that was given to us by my brother and sister-in-law. I dreamed about the doctor shouting in cinematic style, "It's a…!" Boy or girl mattered not but oh, just to know! During this timeframe, it was not common for ultrasounds to be completed in order to know the baby's gender before birth.

What I wanted most of all was my moment, that moment when you get to hold your baby for the first time. The anticipation of feeling the warmth of another life so close to my heart—it was almost unbearable. I wanted to breathe in the smell of my baby, our baby, this new life we had created, and to place my hand gently on the baby's back, close my eyes, and feel those first new breaths of life enter and leave our newborn's chest. That's the moment I dreamed about, a memory I wanted to be able to cherish forever!

On our way to the hospital, we called my parents and Kirk's parents. Since the due date was still eight weeks away and it wasn't my parents' first time at being grandparents, they said to call them once we knew more. I'm sure they thought we would stay a couple of hours and the doctors would send me home. With Kirk's parents, this was going to be their first grandchild, and it didn't matter what time of night. Nothing would stop Brenda from coming to the hospital.

When I was admitted into the new women's wing, I thought it looked more like a hotel than a hospital. The furnishings were beautiful dark wood with nice linens on the bed. It was a new concept to deliver the babies in the same room you were admitted to.

Kirk tried to sleep awhile on the fold-out bed but looked visibly uncomfortable, while Brenda kept me company in between contractions. As I laid in the bed looking across the room at him, my thoughts went back to our high school years when I would see him in the halls at school…a simple glance at each other, a smile to one another as our paths crossed. Now several years later we were together…starting our family.

Just the day before, I had been at the doctor's office. I had been having contractions, and my "motherly instinct" told me it was time, which I'd insistently relayed to the doctor.

Since I was eight weeks early, the doctor assumed my contractions were not the real thing. He checked the position of the baby, and the baby was not face down. At that point, we discussed that if the baby did not turn itself into the proper position for delivery, a C-section would be in order. I was upset by the possibility of having a C-section rather than a "normal" delivery.

Now, a few hours later, I found myself at the hospital waiting, once again, for the doctor. I kept wondering throughout the night, *When is the doctor going to get here?* I was definitely ready.

Morning finally arrived, and the doctor must have been on the premises because suddenly the nurses started to get busy. One came in to do measurements on my belly to estimate how big the baby had grown. Another came in to see if the baby had turned. It had not. I was also required to have a sonogram, since my due date was still weeks away.

After the doctor reviewed the data gathered from the sonogram and from the monitors throughout the night, he came in with the news, "It appears the lungs are developed enough, so it is safe to deliver. Since you've agreed to the C-section, the nurses will get you set up, and I'll see you in the operating room."

Once the epidural was inserted, the meds began to take effect and my legs became heavy. I was wide awake but I wasn't able to feel from my waist down.

Kirk decided he didn't want to be in the room during the delivery since I was having a C-section. I was so upset. This moment had arrived, I was anxious and excited to see our baby together for the first time, and I was scared to be alone. The nurse must have seen "dads-to-be" make this same decision and knew the emotions "moms-to-be" were feeling. She came into our room, laid a set of scrubs on the bed, and said to Kirk, "Well, if you don't change, I guess this mom will have to do it alone." She then walked out with me as I was being pushed down the hall to the delivery room.

Because I was having surgery for the delivery, I had to go to the operating room instead of staying in the room where we had been admitted. As they wheeled me into the OR, everything was bleached out by all the bright fluorescent lighting. The room's incongruent nature became unsettling. I remember a tear rolling down my check because I was alone.

Then suddenly I felt a hand grab my hand. It was Kirk with that smile I had seen for years. I found it so comforting and was now ready for our moment. The doctor reappeared once again and began to prepare my womb for the incision. All I wanted was to see my baby, with Kirk there by my side.

I never felt the cut, but from looking at Kirk's face, I knew it had happened. He kept looking over the drape they had put up. I knew what was coming next, and I held my breath as I waited for those words, *"It's a…!"*

But those words never came.

I suddenly detected urgency, and the doctor's voice echoed in the room, "We've got a problem!" Kirk quickly sat down on the stool beside me, and our eyes locked on each other. But this time, it was a look of fear that we shared.

Trying to imagine the worst, I asked, "Does it have all its fingers and toes?"

My question was met with an emphatic, "Yes." Although appreciating the answer, I was not reassured. I looked at Kirk, and his reddish-blond hair was furrowed along the top of his brow. He was now standing up, motionless, staring at the other side of the drape. His hand in mine turned cold and lifeless as he tried to make sense of what we were experiencing.

I couldn't seem to grasp what was going on and insistently asked, "Well, is it a boy or a girl?"

The doctor ended a pause that seemed to last for hours. "I don't know."

Hopeful Reflections

Feeling Out of Control

Thanking God is hard when your life feels increasingly out of control. Whenever I feel this way, I am always reminded of Ephesians 5:20, "Always giving thanks to God the Father for everything, in the name of our Lord Jesus Christ."

When we feel we have lost all control over certain circumstances in our lives, it is so easy to be consumed by the need to control every minute detail of what is happening. Our unanswered questions and lack of clarity can put a chokehold on our lives, leaving us stuck in our tracks.

When this happens, it is important for us to shift our need to control to our need for Him—the One who never changes, who walks with us through all our storms, and who provides clarity and direction when we don't know what to do.

Take Action:

Today, to help regain some sense of control, think of two things for which you can be thankful. Maybe it's something as simple as being able to eat a meal or have a conversation with someone that provided a distraction to your current situation. Work hard and find two moments in your day that you can be grateful for and write them down.

Tomorrow, before you end your day, do the same thing. This record will help you remember in the days to come that not every moment has been bleak. To find your refuge in an unshakable God, you must first begin with gratitude as your way of worship.

"Therefore, since we are receiving a kingdom that cannot be shaken, let us be thankful, and so worship God acceptably with reverence and awe."
HEBREWS 12:28

"Let the peace of Christ rule in your hearts, since as members of one body you were called to peace. And be thankful."
COLOSSIANS 3:15

Prayer:
Dear Lord, the last thing I want to do today is find something to be grateful for as my mind and heart are consumed with what is happening around me. I have lost control of everything, and I don't know what I am supposed to do next. Even though I may not be able to feel You with me right now, I am thankful I can depend on Your faithfulness and Your Word, which promises You will never leave us nor forsake us. Please step into my life and guide my every thought, emotion, word, and action so that Your will and purpose for me might become evident. In Jesus's name I pray, Amen.

Your Reflections

_____

_____

_____

_____

_____

_____

_____

_____

_____

_____

_____

_____

_____

_____

_____

_____

_____

_____

Chapter 2

The Cradle

Seeking Closure

Within seconds, a host of medical personnel entered the operating room and surrounded the lower half of my bed. Our baby wasn't being lifted up past the drape.

"What is going on? Someone tell me!"

Finally, I saw Kirk's head slowly turn toward me. As his eyes met mine, without a word spoken, he communicated that we were experiencing every parent's worst nightmare, and I began to shake with fear.

Words, so many words that I didn't understand. Our doctor began to describe in medical terms what was going on. Doctors and nurses, NICU specialists, beeps, respirators—it was all white noise. What did it mean? But suddenly no one was talking to me; they weren't even looking at me anymore.

My only thought was, *This can't be happening...why can't I see my baby?* My heart was pounding so hard I could feel the bed shake. I didn't know how much time had passed, but the room suddenly felt dark, although the lighting hadn't changed.

As I became more and more insistent, the uncontrollable shaking progressed. I tried so hard to lift myself up out of the bed, but my lower body was paralyzed due to the meds; all I could do was demand to see my baby. They had placed the baby to the right of my bed, but the room had become so crowded I couldn't see anything. I couldn't see our baby because everyone else was gathered around.

Finally, I saw the head, moving and alive. What little relief I felt quickly dissolved as the medical staff continued to throw words at me that didn't make any sense. Soon, I saw the rest of that tiny figure; it was...all wrapped in gauze. I looked back to my left, and Kirk was no longer beside me.

As I insisted on the baby being brought to me, the doctors and nurses attempted to reason that it wasn't possible. They finally decided to end our debate by showing me why. I raised my head to get a good look at our child. All other motion and thought ceased to exist as I watched a nurse unwrap the gauze around the trunk of my baby to expose a large cavity full of tiny organs and parts of the body never meant to be seen.

"I don't understand. What are you saying?"

As I reached out to try and bridge the gap between me and a tiny hand, the baby was whisked out of the room. My hand was left empty, shaking with sudden grief. I was overwhelmed, in shock, and had no comprehension of what had just taken place.

Meanwhile, the rest of our extended family anxious-ly awaited the news of their grandchild. My parents had arrived once they knew a delivery was taking place, and Kirk's parents were there as well. Kirk left me and took his long walk toward the waiting room. He had to gather his thoughts on how he was going to tell both sets of grandpar-ents something that he himself couldn't even grasp.

No husband. No baby. I was utterly alone, lying in the messy and chaotic operating room, trying to make sense of what was happening.

A nurse soon came in and gave me medicine to stop the shaking. But I fought it every step of the way. I was still waiting for my moment, my cherish-able moment.

Straining to keep my eyes open with whatever might I had left, I heard a voice telling me the baby had to leave the hospital but that I could see my baby right before the ambulance arrived to take it to Children's Medical Center. This meant two very different things in my mind and in the mind of the nurse who explained it to me. I thought a tiny baby swaddled in a blanket would be handed to me to hold. Within a few minutes, some type of cart was wheeled in. A nurse told me it was a portable incubator. As I focused on the box, I realized that locked inside the transparent walls was my baby.

This was not the way this was supposed to go!

Even with my greatest effort, I could only raise my body up just enough to slide my hand through one of the cutouts made in the incubator's wall. I touched my baby's tiny hand for the first time and didn't want to let go.

Within minutes of saying, "I love you," my baby was once again taken from me. Every moment I sensed my child getting farther and farther away from me. My arms were empty, aching, and longing for the gift of which they had been robbed.

A great fight for life was being waged within that tiny soul, and there was nothing I could do. My baby and I were both so helplessly alone.

Eventually I was wheeled down a hallway toward my room. My already broken heart experienced even more pain as I observed all the festive doors displaying pink and blue wreaths and balloons and inhaled the bittersweet scent of roses and star-gazer lilies. My body cringed with each burst of cheer and laughter that erupted from strangers who were oblivious to the despair that lingered in the hall as I passed their rooms.

I had hoped to find some relief from the celebration of other people's cherished moments when I arrived at my room. As I was helped into bed by the nurse, my eyes immediately went to the cradle sitting empty next to my bed.

When she saw the mortified look on my face, the nurse jerked with the realization of the impact this moment had on me. Her apologies fell on deaf ears as all I could do was wonder if our cradle at home would remain empty as well.

Hopeful Reflections

Trusting in God's Plan

"Be patient, then, brothers, until the Lord's coming.
See how the farmer waits for the land to yield
its valuable crop and how patient he is for the autumn
and spring rains. You too, be patient and stand firm,
because the Lord's coming is near."
JAMES 5:7-8

During these emotional times, I longed for closure. I wanted the bad news to end. Nothing had gone as I had planned. The way I'd imagined the delivery of our child would go, seeing my child in the baby bed in my hospital room, and going home in a few short days was not the way it happened. Doctors were uncertain our baby would survive the ride to Children's Medical Center. Even if so, we had no guarantee the cradle waiting at home for us would be used.

My personality is one in which everything has to be "in order" and everything has to go according to "the plan." Whatever is written down and planned then has to be checked off the list, or else I don't have closure. With the birth of my baby, there was nothing I could check off my list.

Maybe you can relate to me in this. Because of my list-making, I can sometimes grow impatient with God's timing. I try to get Him to follow my timeline, but nothing is more futile than trying to tell God how you want your life to play out. God doesn't work according to our "to-do" lists.

God has a plan for each of us, and the Bible says His plan is much better than our own. We may not agree; we may not understand it, but when we are patient in following God's plan, as James tells us, we will come to realize that God only wants the best for us and that His timeline is perfect.

It is God's design that we don't know what the future holds; however, we can be confident in Him who has planned our future, and we can face each situation with the assurance that God is walking through it with us. Closure only comes when we release that circumstance into God's hands.

Take Action:

Ask God to help you trust in His perfect plan and timeline so that you can yield your best fruit yet! Don't grow impatient with God. Instead, trust in His plan, have patience, and discover how truly valuable the crop is that God has in store for you.

Prayer:

Lord, I do not understand Your plan, but help me trust in You. Give me guidance and direction as I seek You in the days ahead. Let me feel Your presence as I relinquish myself to Your plan. In Jesus's name I pray, Amen.

Your Reflections

_____

_____

_____

_____

_____

_____

_____

_____

_____

_____

_____

_____

_____

_____

_____

_____

_____

_____

_____

_____

_____

_____

_____

_____

_____

_____

_____

_____

_____

_____

_____

_____

_____

_____

_____

_____

_____

_____

_____

Chapter 3

A Polaroid

Longing for Peace

Kirk, his parents, and my dad headed straight to the children's hospital to be with our baby while my mother stayed with me. A rush of well-intentioned support occupied my time throughout the day. Awkward phone calls and hospitable yet lumbering visits from friends were certainly well appreciated but did little to calm my fears and bring peace to my grieving heart. I still had no answers. I wanted to crawl into a fetal position and just sleep so I couldn't feel the heartache anymore.

Whenever I got the courage to ask anyone what they had heard, the looks on their faces and the tone of their voices revealed a fear, a dark chasm which no one dared cross. Within hours of birth, my baby was facing a critical surgery. Not even the doctors could predict whether or not my baby would survive. I felt that I too was on that same edge of death.

Twenty-four hours earlier, everything had been right with the world. It's shocking how quickly life as we know it can change. Every plan we envisioned in our hearts and minds for the next twenty years, from first words and first steps to first grade and beyond, were now teetering between the delicate balance of life and death. There is no conceivable way to plan or prepare for something like this. Everything had changed.

At one indiscernible point during the day, a member of the medical staff came in and said the X-rays, examinations, and tests had been evaluated. Then he began speaking in a language I did not understand, repeating words like cloacal exstrophy, omphalocele, malformed pubic rami and exstrophy of the bladder, lipomeningocele, tethered spinal cord, ventricular septal defect, and vater syndrome.

"What do those words mean?"

Through several rounds of questions and answers, I came to understand the abdominal area of my newborn was not fully developed. The bladder was split in half, the pelvic bones were not fused together, and the abdominal area was completely exposed, which left the organs outside the body. Of those organs, the colon was not functional, there were spinal problems, and a heart defect had been found.

This was my first child. In the history of pregnancies, mine was the best. I felt better during my pregnancy than I had at any other point in my life! No morning sickness, full of energy and life, and beaming with the glow of motherhood. If I could, I would have stayed pregnant forever. I loved it! How could an experience so wonderful turn into such foreboding uncertainty?

Late that evening, I finally received a phone call with some information that did not have to be translated by someone who knew medical terminology. My precious baby, in a hospital across town, had survived the first surgery. That news alone lifted such a weight from my heart. I was also elated to know that during the operation, the doctors had discovered an ovary, which meant that I had a little girl. To hear those words at last, just to know, brought me some peace. I found myself in awe at how I could love someone so much that I'd never even had the chance to hold.

After the phone call, I laid in my bed and pictured her little face and wrapped my arms around the thought of her. I physically ached to hold her, to comfort her, to nurture her—to be a mother and to whisper her name in her tiny ear, my little Ragan.

Her first surgery was quite an undertaking. I later discovered that Kirk had confronted the doctor prior to beginning Ragan's surgery, concerned that he was not properly rested to perform such delicate tasks. He had overheard nurses talking about the surgeon not getting any rest between surgeries and the amount of time he had been in surgery prior to being assigned this new case.

The surgeon then explained to Kirk that he was not the one performing the surgery but that God was the one who worked through his hands to perform the surgery. My heart felt another lift in hearing that we had a Christian surgeon who relied on God to give his best performance during Ragan's surgery.

Seven months ago, when we realized we were pregnant, we diligently sought and interviewed doctors until we found the one we felt was right for us. Now, with so many specialized procedures needed for Ragan, we did not have the luxury of getting to know the doctors, of interviewing them, of building a trust with them that we felt we needed. Everything had to happen so fast, and we were forced to trust complete strangers with the fragile life of our baby girl. This left us feeling completely out of control in regard to our baby's care.

As skilled as each of those doctors were, each surgery left us with no guarantees. Would Ragan survive until it was time for the next surgery, and if she did, would she survive the surgery itself? Not even the quality of life for Ragan could be predicted or guaranteed. Everything, each step of the way, remained fearfully unknown.

Recovering from the C-section meant I had a longer hospital stay than other new moms. I recall one evening being told that a friend of ours was just down the hall and had delivered their baby a few hours earlier. We decided to walk down to say hello and to congratulate them. I felt so awkward going into the room without our baby to show but knew we needed to be happy for them. As I sat there looking at their child, our friend handed her to me. As I held her, I became full of emotions and had to give the baby back and quickly leave the room. My eyes were full of tears. I was holding a newborn, but it wasn't mine.

I dreaded the mid-morning parade of check-outs as mothers would be wheeled past my room. They would each coo over their newborns nestled in their arms. Following behind would typically be one of the grandparents, I presumed, along with the new dad, carrying soft blankets, newborn diapers, infant toys that rattled and squished, and festive balloons tied to a cart full of pink or blue flowers—

so much enthusiasm and circumstance paraded outside my door as mothers and babies got to go home together.

A friend of my brother and sister-in-law had come by to check on me. He had been by the children's hospital and taken a picture of Ragan to bring to me. Time stood still as I looked at the picture for the first time. I couldn't take my eyes off of it. I'm sure he didn't realize how much I appreciated him for taking the time to take a picture. None of our family and friends who had been to see Ragan had thought to take a picture for me. It gave me something to hold on to and look at, especially as I saw others being discharged.

We didn't have the technology then that we have now, so all I had was a Polaroid of my tiny Ragan, with her face barely visible through all the tubes and medical tape.

Hopeful Reflections

Finding Your Peace in Him

*"Do not be anxious about anything,
but in everything, by prayer and petition,
with thanksgiving, present your requests to God."*
PHILIPPIANS 4:6

Prayer is simply a conversation. It is the most important line of communication you have and should take top priority over conversations with your spouse, doctor, employer, children, and even your best friend.

Although you may have specific people in your life who are there to offer you love, support, encouragement, guidance, healing, security, and community, there is only One who can provide all these and more. God is the most influential force in our lives, yet sadly, He seems to be the one we turn to least. We fail to utilize the full power that a conversation with God provides.

No matter what is going on in your life, you will experience chaos, unrest, and an absence of peace if your line of communication to God has fallen silent. Whether you have prayed all your life or you are just now being introduced to prayer, take time today to make that call to God. You can be assured that He will always be on the other end of that line, and He is the source of the peace you need in your heart to make it through one more day.

Take Action:

Prayers are not meant to be complicated. Today, practice repeating the simplest of prayers. As a conversation between you and the Giver of all love, hope, and peace, simply say, "Help." Alternate that with saying "Thank you," as you find even the smallest things to be grateful for throughout your day.

Prayer:

Heavenly Father, we thank You for being our help and our strength in times of trouble and uncertainty. Strengthen our faith in You so that we do not waiver in our tough times and so we can find Your peace in even the toughest of circumstances. Amen!

Your Reflections

Chapter 4

Consuming Pain

Desiring Comfort

As the days went by, the lively tones and echoes of other mothers calling relatives and friends over the phone periodically drifted into my room. They were relaying, more often than not, their cherish-able moment to whomever was on the other end of the line. On my phone, the numbers for Children's Medical Center were the most worn. Hour after hour I would call, hoping for an update.

My world became so focused on what was happening with Ragan that everyone else became a nonexistent blur. I was especially oblivious to how Ragan's condition was affecting other members of my family. In my small world, it was just Ragan and I—no one else was recovering from a distressing C-section, no one else ached of loneliness, no one else was confined to a hospital room, and no one understood me, my anger, my grief, my fear, or my all-encompassing pain.

The person closest to understanding the state of mind I was in was my mother. She never left the hospital and stayed with me around the clock. Despite her being there, I still felt the need to be strong, to handle the visitors, and to repeatedly explain the same precarious story to new faces. This was my cross to bear, and I became frustrated with my mother when I would overhear her in the hall explaining what we knew about Ragan and preparing them for the visit prior to seeing me. I was really bothered by that because I was not in control.

I failed to see that Mom was hurting as well. She not only had a new granddaughter she was unable to see or hold but also had a daughter lying in a hospital bed enduring enormous amounts of physical and emotional pain while she helplessly stood by. In the only way she knew how, she did her best to protect me from having to constantly relive the fear that surrounded Ragan's birth and current condition. Instead of thanking her, I lashed out. It wasn't until years later I realized the pain she must have felt, the helplessness.

Kirk was experiencing his own pain and uncertainties as well. He now had two members of his immediate family who needed him. Since he knew my mother was with me, he stayed at the children's hospital to be closer to Ragan. The doctors were relying on him to make quick decisions regarding Ragan's care. The pressure on him was enormous. Since I couldn't be there with Kirk and Ragan, I wasn't being included in important conversations regarding Ragan's life. As I heard updates and the results of decisions that Kirk had to make, I felt resentful that I wasn't included and even more powerless in my role as a new mom.

Even though Kirk knew the most about Ragan's condition, he had great difficulty relaying the information to me. I later came to understand that he simply didn't know how to deal with the pain he saw on my face when he tried to talk. It hurt him too deeply. So, to avoid facing yet another problem he couldn't fix or handle, he avoided me. I could feel his purposeful avoidance, and instead of attempting to understand why, it only fueled the anger and resentment I felt. I wrongly assumed he was maliciously keeping information from me that I so badly needed to hear.

The hospital gave every couple a nice "dinner for two" in their room before being discharged to go home. They served the dinner by candlelight and started the dinner with a nice bottle of wine. I anxiously waited for Kirk to get to the hospital for our dinner. He had come by each day to check on me but wouldn't stay long so that he could be at the children's hospital with Ragan. Still moving slowly from the C-section, I had worked hard that afternoon to take a shower and put makeup on so that I looked presentable for our evening alone.

This would be the first time we were together without friends or family. I needed to be with him, to be held by him, and to be reassured that everything was going to be okay. I needed his strength and confidence that he always displayed. As I heard the door opening, I glanced up with a smile to greet him, and as he walked in, I soon saw he was not alone.

I immediately wanted to cry. My time with Kirk was not going to be how I had thought it would be, and I was not prepared for it.

A friend had decided to come with him to see me and then to go with him to the hospital to see Ragan. Although I was happy to see our friend, I was disappointed not to be alone with Kirk. I didn't realize that Kirk didn't want to be alone with me…he feared that he would not be strong for me and that it would be an evening full of emotions.

After not having the evening with my husband that I had been so looking forward to, I began to fear that all of my life, from now on, would be different from what I had hoped.

Kirk's mother and I, through the years, had developed a uniquely deep bond. Brenda and I shared so much of our lives with one other. However, during this most difficult time yet, she disappeared. I found myself needing her and became upset, wondering why she had abandoned me.

Being consumed by my own circumstances and pain, I couldn't comprehend the needs of others. My mother-in-law needed to be with her son and her grandbaby across town. After a few days had passed, she felt it was okay to leave Kirk's side and come visit me. As soon as Brenda entered the room, our eyes locked, and we each exchanged in emotion what words simply couldn't express. We spent our first long moment together shedding tears onto each other's shoulders. Once our initial outpouring of tears subsided, words were still hard to find. Her face relayed the severity of Ragan's situation and that Ragan's survival was still uncertain.

Finally, the day had come; it was a Saturday when I was released from the doctor's care. Numb and in a foggy, new world of so many uncertainties, I showered and dressed in anticipation of being able to see my baby Ragan. The nurse arrived with the wheelchair as the check-out procedure dictated, but my departure did not have the splendor and circumstance that the other moms were able to experience. My baby was not in my arms, and there was no celebratory parade to the car. Every streamer and wreath that filled doorways I passed as we left added to the pain of my broken heart. As my mom helped me to the car we shared no words. I felt so empty, and instead of heading home with a baby safely strapped into a car seat, I headed to yet another hospital.

Hopeful Reflections

When Your Soul Cannot Find Rest

"I make known the end from the beginning, from ancient times, what is still to come. I say: My purpose will stand, and I will do all that I please."
ISAIAH 46:10

Often in life you'll go through things that you won't understand until years later. I had no idea why I had experienced the circumstances of Ragan's birth until long afterward when I was able to visit other families in crisis. In making hospital visits, I ministered with parents who oftentimes had just received news that the cancer their child was enduring was terminal and that no additional medical treatment was going to help. Understandably, the family found themselves in shock as they tried to reconcile what was happening.

Often in situations like this, we feel a deep anguish that pulses in our soul, and it seems to banish any sign of the peace and comfort we once knew. We struggle with the hope for a miracle while trying to grasp the cold hard facts of a prognosis.

It is important that we don't dwell on the question, "Why me?" but instead cover ourselves in the promises of God's Word as we release our anguish into His hands. This is the only way you or I, mere mortals, can cope in a situation like this. The Scripture refers to God's purpose and plan for our lives and that even when we feel deep pain and unrest, we can rest in the fact that His purpose will still be accomplished.

This is a deep thought. Pain may be a part of the growth process as we watch God's plan unfold.

Earlier in Isaiah, the passage says, "But those who hope in the LORD will renew their strength. They will soar on wings like eagles; they will run and not grow weary, they will walk and not be faint" (Isa. 40:31). We must learn to embrace the situation we are in so that we may grow spiritually, allowing God to be glorified through us as He outshines our circumstances.

One thing we need to be sure to distinguish here is the word *embrace* and how it is used. We generally think of *embrace* as being associated with a loving, positive experience. However, when we use the term in regard to embracing a difficult circumstance, it simply means that we keep our minds and hearts open to God, allowing Christ to draw us closer to Him as He reveals Himself within the situation.

There is nothing to fear in that hospital room as I visit families going through such hardship. The real miracle of healing is taking place as their hearts lean on the God who created their child. Over time, it is amazing to see them begin to understand and accept that one day, their child will be standing whole and will be in the arms of Jesus in heaven.

"O God, our times are in your Hand" (Psalm 31:15, paraphrase). Truly, none of us knows the number of our days, nor can we fully understand God's will and purpose for our lives. But we can be sure that the God of creation is fulfilling His intentions through His love for us.

Take Action:

First, be sure you are keeping up with your gratitude list, finding two things each day you can be thankful for before you end your day.

Next, take some time to be alone. Step to the hospital's chapel if you need to or even outside for a moment to collect your thoughts. Instead of allowing your mind to conjure up all the worst-case scenarios, identify some of your genuine, specific concerns. What is it that is consuming your mind, causing such unrest? Write them down.

Take some time to pray over those thoughts, and if you want, talk about them with a mentor, chaplain, pastor, or someone you trust. Prayer helps control those thoughts that leave us feeling helpless and can open our eyes to action steps we can take to be proactive about the issues within our control.

Prayer:

Dear Lord, my thoughts are robbing me of rest in You, and I need refuge. Please help me release that which I cannot control and guide my way as I act on those issues that are within my control. In Jesus's name I pray, Amen.

Your Reflections

_____

_____

_____

_____

_____

_____

_____

_____

_____

_____

_____

_____

_____

_____

_____

_____

_____

_____

_____

_____

_____

_____

_____

_____

_____

_____

_____

_____

_____

_____

_____

_____

_____

_____

_____

_____

_____

_____

_____

Chapter 5

The Outsider

Void of Position

Although I protested, my family had a wheelchair waiting for me at the door when I arrived at Children's Medical Center. As I went to the third floor Intensive Care Unit, I was trying to focus on the positive aspects of being able to see Ragan. However, my heart pounded with sorrowful regret in knowing that she was here first—brought here alone, and that I was not here to hold and comfort her through her pain.

As we entered the elevator, my breathing became fast, and I took deep breaths to slow it down. When the elevator doors opened, I entered what appeared to be a messy living room with an abnormal number of recliners and coffee tables, all covered with the smelly remnants of fast-food meals and yesterday's newspapers. This was the waiting room where multiple families lived, including mine, who had children fighting for life beyond the double doors where few could actually go.

My family greeted others in the room with friendly familiarity, asking about their children by name.

After leaving the wheelchair, I awkwardly stood in the doorway's shadow. I noticed a board on the wall where people checked out by listing their child's name, their name, and their phone number so they could be reached if something changed with their child. My name was noticeably absent from the list of Ragan's family members since I had not been at the hospital with her yet.

My family had had almost a week to get to know the others who were living in the waiting room. They also knew the protocol of what to say, where to sit, and how to check in for updates. Everyone in this room had a place except me. I didn't dare try to sit down for fear of taking someone's spot. No one knew me and acted as such—I was the outsider.

The ICU allowed patients to have visitors, but limited them to two at a time, every three hours. Since I was so anxious to see Ragan, we called ahead to make sure I could get in to see her upon my immediate arrival. After finding our "family spot" in the waiting area where I put my belongings, Kirk led me to the area where the next phase would take place.

The ritual of visiting your child in the ICU is a detailed and awkward protocol. It involves scrubbing your hands and lower arms for three minutes with cleanser, thoroughly rinsing under hot water, and then turning the water off with your knee. There is a huge emphasis placed on the importance of not touching faucets with your hands. All of this, including the donning of a paper gown, is much easier said than done.

I had entered another world in which I didn't know the language or the lay of the land. I felt detached from not only my family but also myself. I was so focused on getting to see Ragan, I could barely understand all the rules people were spouting my way. I followed the directions given and hoped I was doing them correctly. In order to get through these unbearable moments, I did my best to shove my feelings into an abyss in my heart so I could be strong for my baby.

The ICU was an open room with several children whose space was divided by hospital curtains—some opened, some closed. I was so terrified to look around at the others for fear of what I would see. I just wanted to see Ragan.

Nothing could have prepared me for this moment.

I had spent the last few days holding a Polaroid picture of her, but it wasn't until I saw all the machines attached to the tubes coming out of her body that the severity of her condition registered. Tears began to roll down my cheeks as I intently gazed at her face. She was so beautiful. My arms were screaming to hold her, but I couldn't.

The nurse started explaining what each tube and wire did and how the medical staff was taking care of her. She certainly meant well, but I didn't hear a word she said. I couldn't take my eyes off of Ragan. I touched her little hands, and the tears continued to stream down my face. My body convulsed with the love that was pouring out of me and the intense desire I had to care for my baby girl.

I felt as though I wanted to scream and fall to the ground with emotion. But all of a sudden, even with tears streaming down my face, I just felt empty, as though I couldn't show any emotion at all.

Before I knew it, the nursing staff was pulling me out of the room. Our visiting shift was over. I was livid as I thought, *It's been five days since I delivered my baby, and you are kicking me out after only a few minutes of being with her for the first time!* I was crushed.

A nurse instructed me to go back to the waiting room, which I did begrudgingly. When I entered, time stood still as I collected the pained looks on the faces looking back at me. There were no words that could be said, and they knew there was no comfort that could be offered to appease what I had just seen.

How is she going to react? That's what I imagined was in everyone's minds. *Is she going to fall apart?* I just wanted this nightmare to end. A week ago, things were normal. Why couldn't we just get back to that?

Staring at all those awkward expressions in the waiting room, I couldn't help thinking, *With a room full of loved ones, why don't I feel loved?*

Hopeful Reflections

How to Find Our Place When We Feel Lost

*"Though he stumble, he will not fall,
for the LORD upholds him with his hand."*
PSALM 37:24

We have all been derailed by the circumstances of life, and many are there right now. When our life doesn't seem to fit into the picture-perfect mold that we have cast for ourselves, we hear a voice in our head listing everything we have done wrong. That list of faults is then accompanied by guilt, remorse, shame, and withdrawal.

God gave us His Holy Spirit to guide us into truth, and to convince us of His righteousness. He offers us forgiveness and brings us into right standing with God despite all we've done wrong. We can then put our guilt and shame aside and live in the truth of His forgiveness.

We all fall. Some falls cause a scrape or a bruise that takes some time to heal. But sometimes when we experience a fall or a circumstance that we just can't understand or comprehend, we are overwhelmed with brokenness that doesn't seem like it can ever heal.

God understands, and He is not there to condemn you with further guilt and misery. He is there to help you up, to give you HOPE, and to give you the strength to endure all that you encounter in your life.

Lamentations 3:22 says, "Because of the LORD's great love we are not consumed, for his compassions never fail." He is there to encourage you and to help you recognize His hand in your life, despite the storms that may be surrounding you.

Take Action:

No matter what you have going on in your life right now, take a moment to remember times when you knew where you stood. Think back on times that were good, when through God's mercies, you, your family, or your friends pulled through.

Bring in some reinforcements as well and ask those around you to tell you stories of times when they felt lost and didn't know what their position was in life and God showed His faithfulness in their lives. God's faithfulness in the past is what paves the way to our HOPE in the future, knowing that God will never leave us or forsake us, especially in our time of need.

Prayer:

Dear Lord, You know the burdens we carry, and it is so easy to add despair, guilt, and hopelessness to our load. Please help us know that the negative and destructive thoughts we have are not from You. Please cover us with Your mercy and grace and remind us that because of Your Son and His sacrifice for us, we are children of God. Help us to remember that You are with us always, guiding us into the light of Your truth. Thank you for being our HOPE. In Jesus's name we pray, Amen.

Your Reflections

_____

_____

_____

_____

_____

_____

_____

_____

_____

_____

_____

_____

_____

_____

_____

_____

_____

_____

_____

_____

Chapter 6

Abnormally Normal

Our New Normal

When you travel through a storm, you encounter turbulence, rain, thunder and lightning. In the midst of the storm, you begin to wonder if you'll survive, and then just as suddenly, the sky clears, the wind stops howling, and the storm passes. The next day the only evidence you might see is the aftermath of downed tree limbs or debris, or the creeks overflowing with flood waters. A week later when the water has subsided, the grass grows taller and greener and you can look back on the storm with respect and gratitude.

Inside the eye of the storm, however, you cannot see the purpose for the chaos and pain. During the first few weeks after Ragan's birth, each time I thought progress was being made, it seemed to come with its own setbacks. Each day brought new problems and new emotions to work through as we had to continually make decisions regarding Ragan's life. Because Ragan's condition was so rare, it seemed each medical specialist had a different approach or opinion as to what was best regarding her care.

At one point, we were even handed a box of various medical supplies and told to "experiment" with Ragan to see what would work and what wouldn't. Since children did not typically need these types of products, no one could accurately determine what should be used to best care for her. Kirk and I both had to go through special medical training before we could even think about bringing Ragan home.

At this critical juncture, it seemed everyone was abandoning me. Kirk went back to work, and people who had been there every day for the first few weeks eventually stopped coming to visit. Their lives went back to normal. Meanwhile, my days were filled with doctor consultations, hours of sitting in a waiting room, and ridiculous amounts of time washing my hands. It began to sink in that nothing about my life would ever be normal again.

Finally, three weeks after Ragan was born, I got to hold her for the first time. It was during the middle of the night when I couldn't get comfortable in the recliner and I was having trouble sleeping. I went in to check on her in the ICU, and the nurse said it was time that I got to hold my baby girl. They got a rocking chair for me to sit in and a camera for the first picture. It was incredible; time stood still. It was as though no one else was in the room. I didn't hear the medical machines, the other children in the room, or the ICU staff. As I looked at her little hands, feet, legs, arms, ears...every inch of her body, I was amazed at this little miracle and whispered to her that God had a special plan for her.

Being told that Ragan would be in the hospital for at least three months was distressing, but she came home almost a month later. I did not know what the future held for her. The doctors said she would not be able to sit up on her own and perhaps not ever be able to walk. Ragan's struggle to prove them wrong had just begun, even in her first few weeks of life.

I was so ready for our life to feel normal. The very next day after coming home from the hospital, my mother-in-law and I took Ragan to the mall. My father-in-law was protective of Ragan and voiced his concern of her being out in public, but I just wanted to do something that other moms were doing—loading the stroller in the car, driving somewhere without medical staff, unloading the stroller, and pushing my baby around. Upon arriving at the mall, it seemed like I had a small piece of normalcy for a brief moment.

But reality soon set back in once we were home, hooking Ragan up to a feeding pump every few hours and performing various medical steps for her care; this was our "new normal." I did my best to keep her room looking like a baby nursery by cleaning out a hall closet near her room to utilize it as a medical supply closet.

After coming home from the hospital, the weekly doctor's visits began. We had follow-up visits with each doctor who had been assigned to her care. Plans for moving forward began to develop. It seemed that we had just gotten Ragan home and the doctors were already planning the next surgery. After visiting with the neurosurgeon just weeks after coming home, he had already planned that at the age of five months, she would have her first spinal surgery.

Over the next few months as we cared for her daily needs, we were like other parents in that we didn't get much sleep. Although Ragan was taking feedings throughout the day by bottle, at night, she was fed through a feeding tube. This was to get her weight up. We got up every two hours to change the milk in the feeding machine. I can remember talking with other new moms who complained about getting up all through the night to feed their little ones. I would shake my head and think, *At least you are holding your child in the middle of the night while feeding, while I'm changing bags for a feeding tube; if you only knew to appreciate what you have.*

Our days included nursing duties that I had to learn quickly in order to meet Ragan's medical needs. These were so hard to do at times due to the pain that some of them caused her. I had to learn to separate myself from being her mother during these procedures and focus on the medical requirements in order to get through them. It was so hard and emotionally draining.

The first time Ragan's feeding tube came out, I was home alone and it was time for her feeding. I called my next-door neighbor to come over and assist me, and she graciously came and held Ragan while I completed the task. She could not believe that we had to perform these procedures on our little one and commented on how strong I was.

Soon, the day came for us to head back to the hospital for Ragan's first spinal surgery. We spent the first day in the hospital having all sorts of tests run in preparation for the surgery. It was a very long day for Ragan to endure, and we both were ready for bed that night. Kirk had gone home and planned on coming back to the hospital early the next morning prior to the surgery.

Nurses told me they would not be coming in through the night so that we could get some rest for the long day ahead. At around 11:00 p.m., a nurse came into the room to wake me up. She said that a doctor was on the phone wanting to talk with me. I went to the nurses' station, only to find out that there would be no surgery the following day. The anesthesiologist said that Ragan was too small and that she did not feel that Ragan would survive the surgery.

Anger came over me...I could not believe that we had been at the hospital since eight o'clock that morning and it had taken her that long to make this decision. As I hung up the phone, the nurses knew I was very upset. They said we could spend the night and leave in the morning. I insisted on packing up and leaving right then. I was exhausted but had been emotionally ready to endure another surgery, and in an instant, the surgery had been postponed. Looking back now, I didn't realize God's protection of Ragan was in place. I was just so angry and wanted to leave as quickly as I could to go home and sleep in my own bed. For the next few months, we focused on increased feedings to help make Ragan stronger in preparation for surgery.

Over the next couple of months, we got back into a routine. Ragan was meeting her challenges day in and day out. At the age of seven months, she sat up on her own without pillows surrounding her to lean on. Now for her, this was a huge hurdle she had overcome. She had no muscles in her abdominal area, so the doctors had told us she would not be able to sit alone until we had multiple surgeries to pull muscles around from her back area.

I called the doctors to let them know that she was sitting up on her own, and I was told it was impossible for her to be able to do this. So, I did what any proud mother would do. Ragan and I got in the car and drove to the doctor's office to show her accomplishment. As she sat up looking at the doctors with the bright smile God blessed her with, she knew she had accomplished something big, and she was proud; her big brown eyes sparkled with pride. The doctors were amazed.

Over the next two years, our "normal" was managing hospital visits, doctor's office visits, and learning medical steps to better care for her. By the age of two, Ragan had been to the operating room eight times and underwent fifty-two day surgeries.

I often grew tired of trips to the hospital. From the age of one to age two, we were at the hospital every week for day surgery as well as several times for major surgeries. I had gone back to work part time in order to assist with the bills and to allow me some time away from the medical issues. But no one truly understood what was going on inside of me. I felt so alone and as though I had no one to turn to. I was simply going through the motions each day. Kirk was working long hours, and there seemed to be a disconnect between us. We often found ourselves so tired physically and emotionally that neither of us set aside time for the other. This is common in families with children with medical issues.

Ragan's cousin Krystle, who is two months younger, helped her accomplish the impossible. When I did not think Ragan would crawl, Krystle taught her by example. In addition to crawling, Ragan learned to pull herself up on the sofa. I feel she succeeded because Krystle watched from the sofa and encouraged her. Krystle loved Ragan, and even at such a young age, Krystle knew she could help Ragan by encouraging her to do the things she could do.

Shortly after these accomplishments, Ragan conquered yet another obstacle that we didn't think she'd be able to overcome, due to the spinal issues she had.

On Easter morning, Kirk and I were getting ready for church. Money was very tight and we could not afford new outfits, so I had purchased fabric and made dresses for Ragan and myself. I had gotten Ragan dressed, and she was crawling around, waiting on us to get ready. Things seemed to get quiet in the other room where Ragan was playing. As Kirk and I walked into the room to see what she was do-ing, we could not believe our eyes. Ragan was standing up, clapping and smiling. And then it happened… At the age of almost three years old, Ragan took her first steps without our assistance.

Time stood still as Kirk and I embraced and cheered her on with pride in her accomplishment. We shouted with joy, and tears fell from both our eyes. We waited until after church to tell anyone. Upon arrival for Easter family cele-bration, Ragan showed everyone what she could do.

At this time, she still had braces on her little legs and had been going to physical therapy several times a week. But we were still being told that the unknown was ahead of us. I cannot express to you the joy that filled our entire family on this special day. Despite our problems, Kirk and I held these moments close to our hearts. As you can imagine, Easter is very special to us for more than the obvious celebration.

Hopeful Reflections

Finding a New Normal

"Three times I pleaded with the Lord to take it away from me. But he said to me, 'My grace is sufficient for you, for my power is made perfect in weakness.' Therefore I will boast all the more gladly about my weaknesses, so that Christ's power may rest on me. That is why, for Christ's sake, I delight in weaknesses, in insults, in hardships, in persecutions, in difficulties. For when I am weak, then I am strong."
2 CORINTHIANS 12:8–10

The above portion of Paul's letter to the Corinthians has helped me during many difficulties throughout my life, whenever what I considered to be "normal" was challenged in big ways. This isn't something to read once and simply retain for life. For me, I need to be reminded of this lesson time and again, and I find much rest once I am redirected back to this passage.

Although the whole chapter is a passage I've often read, it is the last sentence in verse eight that gets my attention every time. It reminds me that "I am strong when weak."

We often find ourselves asking God for help in our trials and weaknesses, wanting Him to perform a miracle and get us out of the difficulty we are in. We simply want things back to the way they were. When we do not experience deliverance in the way or time we want, it is very easy to get frustrated and lose sight of the bigger picture. Even Paul experienced this. In verse 8, he asked the Lord for special deliverance three times, yet it did not come.

Paul finally realized that God's grace was made strong in his weakness. Don't miss this. It is within our times of trouble that we must be willing to let go of being in charge and let God take over. In times of plenty and in times that are bare, we are merely stewards of what God has given us. We need to allow the ownership privilege to remain with Him and allow God to carry the bulk of our burdens.

When we understand we are merely managers and stewards, we achieve the proper mindset of deferring to the Owner of all things, our ultimate Guide, on what we should do and how we should manage what is on loan to us. When we do this, our mind and attitude can find a most unusual but special kind of "delight" as God's power and grace are able to be displayed in our times of weakness and pain.

Things just don't always go as planned.

When everything, including our relationships, looks and feels different, it can be unsettling. Remember that in a world of unrelenting changes, God is the one who never changes. In His presence, you can face uncertainty with perfect peace.

Look to God's unwavering love and promises for your "new normal," instead of your ever-changing circumstances.

Take Action:

Take a moment to write out the new circumstances and situations weighing heaviest on your mind. Divide them into two columns: things I can control and things I cannot control.

For those things you can control, seek help to find ways to eliminate the burden. For many families going through difficult times, the simple task of mowing the lawn can seem monumental when all your time is spent at the hospital. Be humble enough to ask for help, or if you are able, hire someone to handle it. Ask a family friend or neighbor to help with mail or getting the other siblings to and from school. People are willing to help if they just know what you need.

For those things you cannot control, lift them up to God and pray for the ability to release your desire to control those burdens you were never meant to carry.

Prayer:

Dear Jesus, I know I am holding onto burdens that I was never meant to carry because of things I was never meant to control. Please give me wisdom to know what I can do and release control to You for the things only You can do. Help me navigate these new changes in my life as we find our new normal. In Your name I pray, Amen.

Your Reflections

_____

_____

_____

_____

_____

_____

_____

_____

_____

_____

_____

_____

_____

_____

_____

_____

_____

_____

_____

_____

_____

_____

_____

_____

_____

_____

_____

_____

_____

_____

_____

_____

_____

_____

_____

_____

_____

_____

_____

_____

_____

_____

_____

_____

_____

Chapter 7

Questioning Everything

Yearning for Answers

In the early years after Ragan was born, whenever we found ourselves stuck in a line, rush hour traffic, or a hospital waiting room, there weren't any smart phones or hotspots available to occupy our time. There was only so much you could do while waiting in line or in traffic and only so many magazines you could read in a medical office. I was left with a lot of time and a lot of questions. One of my first questions was, "Why me?"

I grew up in a Christian home and claimed to have faith in God. However, I found myself asking, *Why would the Lord allow a child to be born with so many problems?* The answer was not there. That delivery room changed the entire trajectory of my life, and I saw nothing good coming of it.

Even though I didn't know why at the time, I made it a point to take part in the weekly services that were held in the hospital's chapel when we were admitted. On one particular Sunday morning, the pastor spoke from a passage in the Gospel of John. In his sermon, he talked about when the disciples asked Jesus why a man was born blind. Before He healed the man, Jesus replied, *"That the work of God might be displayed in his life"* (John 9:3).

Somehow, I sensed the answer I was looking for was in that passage. However, that answer left me even more confused, and I was incapable of accepting it. There had to be someone to blame, something I could point to and say, "That is why this has happened."

When Ragan was born and in the earlier years, there weren't support groups for families like there are now. Eventually, the hospital recognized that parents of children with medical issues needed emotional support. Their solution was to start a support group. Although they had good intentions, the group did not have the structure or leadership necessary to make it a productive source of support. I attended the first meeting and, within the first few minutes, it became very clear to me that this was going to be a time of people feeling sorry for themselves. It even seemed to become a competition based on who had the most medically-challenged child. My only thought throughout the meeting was, *What am I doing here?*

Even though I was longing for someone to understand what I was going through, I did not want to be a part of a group like that. I didn't attend another meeting. I decided it was time for me to get involved in church again, and I started going, but because I could not go consistently, I didn't feel like I had a church family. I was still feeling alone.

As a Christian, I was so torn. I knew I was to have faith, but fear was starting to set in, and I felt that if I allowed myself to fear, that meant I was questioning my faith in God. I felt as though I had no one to discuss these feelings with, so I prayed…a lot, asking God to show me scripture to get me through these feelings of fear. Although God had not been a priority in my life prior to this time, He had never left me through the years and continued to show me comfort through His Word. It's not the weight of your faith; it's what you put your faith in that matters most, regardless of how little faith you may have.

Not only did I question my level of fear and faith, I also questioned my support system. During our many hospital stays, I longed for Christian visitors to comfort me by bringing some perspective to what I was going through; but more times than not, their words ended up confusing rather than comforting me. If you've ever been through something like this, you know what I'm talking about. You may have even heard that God never gives us more than we can handle or some other Christian quote that left you shaking your head.

Some people told me, "These things don't just happen; God uses circumstances to punish us," leaving me with plenty of unpleasant questions. If that were true, then what did I do in the past that was causing me to be punished in this way?

Others came by the hospital and tried to combat the suffering with cheer and then they left, never to come again. I have even been told that I needed to hold my head up high because the faith of others will increase based on how I handle every moment. "Don't show suffering—it's a sign of weakness." That's a lot of pressure to put on someone who is hurting!

What I came to understand was that people feel helpless around those in pain—helpless and, maybe at times, guilty that they are not feeling the pain they see you in. Not knowing what to say often leads to a reaction or words that give little comfort to those who are suffering. I know this is not their intent, and it is often hard for those making the visits. That is why a lot of times, they come once to visit and then do not return. Sometimes they make a visit to do a good deed, serving our Lord. But in reality, it was for them to feel good about themselves.

One thing I have learned is to find God's people when you have questions, especially when you are hurting. Seek wise counsel from strong believers. Also, find ways not only to endure but to prevail. One way of doing this is by doing something for others.

"Rejoice with those who rejoice; mourn with those who mourn." (Romans 12:15)

By getting some good, godly comfort through the years from a select group, I now try to pass on to others what I know to be true about God's faithfulness. God will hold you up with His unending mercy. You are not alone through this time of trials.

Hopeful Reflections

His Grace is Sufficient

"Trust in the LORD with all your heart and lean not on your own understanding; in all your ways acknowledge him, and he will make your paths straight."
PROVERBS 3:5-6

The verse above has often brought me peace. I continue to find comfort in knowing Him personally and trusting that He walks the path ahead, creating a better way for me.

Remember—be true to your feelings. Allow the feelings you have to be acknowledged and addressed, but don't stay there. We do not always get the answers we are looking for, and sometimes, we feel like we don't get answers at all. When we have unknown factors in our lives, we can be consumed with the fear of the unknown.

However, God's grace is sufficient for us, but its sufficiency is for only one day at a time. Perhaps God divided time into days and nights so we would have manageable portions of life to handle. I'm not sure, but it makes sense to me!

That is why Jesus told us that tomorrow has its own trouble so do not worry about tomorrow. Focus on just taking care of today. God is working on our behalf, regardless of what or how we are feeling in the moment.

Many Christians believe that our fear shows a lack of faith in God, but what they do not know is how to deal with the fear, which means they are left feeling afraid or helpless in the face of those unknowns. This is often what we feel as parents about our child's health, not knowing what today, tomorrow, or years from now will bring. These unanswered questions can be fraught with fear.

However, we can learn to resist fear when it arises. Second Timothy 1:7 says, *"For God has not given us a spirit of fear, but of power and of love and of a sound mind."*

Fear is one of Satan's favorite ways to gain power over us. To feel fear is not a sin or an act of disobedience, because it's an emotion just like anger or love. We as Christians need to decide what to do with the fear and how to respond to it.

Take Action:

Take some time to look back over your list of things you are thankful for each day. Have you come across anything that first brought you fear that you are now able to give as an offering of thanks?

At the back of your gratitude journal, write down your fears and then put a checkmark on what is a concern for today. Then identify what is a concern for the future.

During your prayer time, ask God to help you keep tomorrow's questions and concerns at bay while He guides you through today.

Prayer:

Dear Father in heaven, please protect my mind from being consumed by questions that I don't have answers to right now. Help me focus my attention on You as You guide me through each step I take and as I focus on today's concerns and leave tomorrow's concerns to You. I trust that You know the answers to any questions I have, and that is sufficient for me. In the name of Jesus I pray, Amen.

Your Reflections

_____

_____

_____

_____

_____

_____

_____

_____

_____

_____

_____

_____

_____

_____

_____

_____

_____

_____

_____

_____

_____

_____

_____

_____

_____

_____

_____

_____

_____

_____

_____

_____

_____

_____

_____

_____

_____

_____

_____

_____

Chapter 8

The Marriage

Void of Communication

To add to the uncertainties of life during that most diffi-cult time, Kirk and I both were overwhelmed with so many unexplainable emotions that it affected the heart of our marriage. We began to experience more and more conflict in our relationship as we each built impenetrable walls be-tween us.

This led to a growing form of distrust that we were not able to overcome. Our inability to communicate with each other was never addressed. We each hid in our own fear and never acknowledged the core of the other's pain.

My marriage was dissolving before my eyes, and no one seemed to notice. I was empty inside and did not feel that I had a purpose in life. Although I had friends and family, I felt as though no one would understand my feelings. On the outside I had it all—a husband, a child, family nearby; I had a nice home and job, and it appeared we had means to have pretty much whatever we wanted, but I was so *alone*. I recall during the first few weeks after Ragan's birth, one of the doctors pulled us aside and explained that he had seen divorces in situations like ours, time after time.

He said we had a choice to pull together and be an incredible testimony for others, or we would eventually grow apart and find ourselves going our separate ways. And that's exactly what happened.

Over the following year, I realized that I didn't have a marriage any longer; I found that we had each gone our separate ways. Our struggles and feelings were not united. As I looked at the man I had fallen in love with several years earlier, I felt as though I had nothing to give him. I felt guilty for giving him a child that had so many medical struggles and guilty that our lives had changed so much.

I knew I would always love him, but because of the pain I had inside, I was struggling to be a wife. My self-worth was gone, and I felt that he didn't love me anymore. I wished I could cry with him beside me, holding me and perhaps crying with me. We didn't share those emotions together. I don't remember ever crying together or talking through Ragan's struggles, which is probably the opposite of what the world thought when they saw us.

On the surface, everyone thought I was so strong and had it all. But inside, I was empty.

Ragan was not to blame for our marriage dissolving. The problem was that we did not direct our focus to God, nor did we communicate with each other. We didn't make joint prayer a priority in our home. We prayed individually but were not united in our efforts. We became focused on ourselves and not on our marriage. Lack of communication and unity often results in fractured marriages. When our children are sick, that becomes our focus, and unfortunately, others we love get lost.

Regardless of the good times Kirk and I shared, we separated and divorced shortly after. We still have a close bond with one another and made a mutual decision that we would be there for Ragan together throughout her life. She is so important to us both, and we want to share her life with each other. I appreciate both of our families for making this a priority for us all.

Oftentimes at the hospital, the staff could not believe that we were not married. Our families united together, and many times, Kirk and I would stay at the hospital together. Ragan has always been our priority, and we were able to continue to focus on her and not on ourselves.

Hindsight is 20/20 and throughout it all I'm sure we both wished we could have made it all work, but we accepted our mistakes and moved on while continuing to operate as a family, which we would always be. We are connected by Ragan, and her life and happiness has always been our priority.

Hopeful Reflections

Protect Your Marriage

"Two are better than one, because they have a good return for their work: If one falls down, his friend can help him up. But pity the man who falls and has no one to help him up!"
<small>ECCLESIASTES 4:9-10</small>

It is important that you make time for yourself to be alone with God *daily*! But, also be united with your spouse and pray together. Prayer is so powerful for your marriage. Prior to your prayer time with each other, allow some time to share with one another what you have been learning during your individual time studying God's Word.

It is also important that both of you are on the same page regarding the status and care of not only your child experiencing the illness or injury but also any other children in the household. Make time to talk, be vulnerable with each other, and share your joys, fears, concerns, and prayers.

Take Action:

Pray with your spouse daily. First Thessalonians 5:17 reads, *"Pray without ceasing."* That means for us to develop a habit of talking with God about everything that is going on in our lives. Our spouse also needs to be a part of this conversation.

As an individual, it will also help keep your marriage strong if you make prayer a part of your day throughout the day. Not just at a specific time of the day but at any time, talk to God. Be His child; it brings Him pleasure hearing your voice.

Keep a running list of questions, comments, appointments, etc., that you need to go over with your spouse. Schedule time at least once a week to get your calendars together, finances together, and list of questions together so you can remain involved in what is going on in each other's lives.

Allow yourself and agree with your spouse that each of you will give each other the time and space needed to grieve for your child's illness and understand that each of you will grieve in different ways.

Prayer:

Dear Jesus, please put a hedge of protection around our relationship and strengthen us as we work to strengthen each other on this journey. In Your name I pray, Amen.

Your Reflections

_____

_____

_____

_____

_____

_____

_____

_____

_____

_____

_____

_____

_____

_____

_____

_____

_____

_____

_____

_____

_____

_____

Chapter 9

Solitude's Hold

Craving Connection

After my divorce, I pulled away from God for a period of time; I was trying to do it all on my own. This is when I began to feel hopeless.

Bills were not getting paid; jobs were hard to keep; frustration and doubt were setting in. Satan was beginning his plan of defeat for me. I knew God was always there with me, but I didn't allow Him to be present in my life.

I began to focus on the negatives and tried to control all that was occurring. Deep down, I knew what needed to be done, but I thought I could do it all myself. Ever since Ragan's birth, I had heard how strong I was and truly started believing that I was strong and didn't need Christ to carry me through the difficult times. These were the times I knew I needed to strengthen my walk with Christ, but I couldn't seem to get out of the deep pit I was in.

Because of being at the hospital so much with Ragan, it was hard maintaining a job, which meant funds were limited. I had grown up learning the importance of a good work ethic, but putting the importance on a job was difficult— missing work, sleepless nights caring for Ragan meant days of weariness and constant fatigue, which led to not being consistent at a job.

God blessed us with a godly couple, Bill and Linda, to be a part of our lives. Linda watched Ragan daily so I could go to work. Ragan became part of their family and had the love of their children, Loderick, Ben, and Stephanie "Sissy."

Although Linda stayed at the hospital during the day, I often had to leave work early in order to get to Ragan as quickly as possible to spend the evening and night with her. I would take a shower and prepare to go to work each morning while in the hospital room, waiting to see the doctors as they made rounds. My life was a roller coaster from day to day, not knowing how Ragan would be doing and making quick changes in my plans so I could be with her for medical visits and during various tests.

The more I tried to work to make enough money for Ragan and me to live on, the more it seemed I needed to be home with her. Again, I was trying to do it all on my own without letting anyone know how much I was struggling financially and emotionally.

There were many times I wondered what Ragan and I were going to eat. Sometimes we had only a loaf of bread and half a jar of peanut butter to get us through until next payday. This had become a normal concern on a weekly basis.

I found myself going to bed hungry at times and not maintaining good nutritional intake. This caused more fatigue and stress on my body and affected daily decisions and my ability to deal with my workload. In the midst of having no food, I tried to make sure Ragan didn't know or feel the struggles we were having. We would have "camp out night" on Fridays and would get our sleeping bags and bring them to the den to watch a movie while eating popcorn for our dinner. Ragan thought it was a treat, but I knew it was simply because we had nothing else to eat and no funds for groceries.

There were so many lonely times at the hospital with Ragan as well as at home with her. Don't misunderstand what I am saying. I was surrounded by family and friends… but I felt so alone and oftentimes desperate.

God is creative and thorough in meeting our needs if we will follow His direction rather than our own. There were many people over the years who simply said, "I would like to do this for you." Had they asked me what I needed at that time, I'm not sure I would have known what to ask for. But God was directing them with their offers, and my needs were met.

For example, as a single mother trying to maintain a job and spending every moment I could at the hospital, I was often drained emotionally and physically, as well as financially. Ragan's babysitter Linda never asked me when she needed to come and stay during the day so I could work. She simply arranged the time with Ragan's MaMa, and they would work out a schedule to rotate individuals to assist. Brenda, Ragan's MaMa, and Linda knew the needs that had to be met and made it happen. Through these precious women operating under God's direction, it brought me peace and renewal of strength to return from work each day to spend the evenings and nights with Ragan during our many visits to the hospital.

Through the years, we have been lifted up through prayer by many. We have received cards, meals, even firewood for the winter. Many times, I did not know how I was going to buy groceries for the week. I recall one time, without my sharing with anyone the dilemma I was in, my doorbell rang. When I opened the door, there was no one there, but as I looked down at the porch, there were bags and bags of groceries for Ragan and I. Tears began to run down my face as I brought the groceries into the house to put them away.

There have been so many times that God has provided for us. Oftentimes, people are looking for the "big" things to do for others, but if there is one thing I have learned about caring for others, it's often the "little" things that are needed the most and make the "biggest" impact on those in need.

One Christmas, Ragan was not allowed to eat anything by mouth because she was being fed by a feeding tube. I didn't know how we were going to handle the family Christmas meal. When we arrived at my mother and father's home, my mom had it all figured out. She had made ice cubes with green and red food coloring. Ragan could eat ice and drink water or juice, but that was the only intake she could have. So, my mother made that available for her to have, and with it being the Christmas colors, Ragan thought that was really neat.

My mother had also arranged for Ragan to go to a neighbor's home when it came time for the family meal.

This retired woman who lived next door had a doll collection. What I found so remarkable was that my mother had thought through Ragan's needs and had made arrangements accordingly. When my niece Rebecca found out that Ragan was going next door, she volunteered to go with her and eat privately when she returned. Rebecca is a few years older than Ragan and has looked after her needs through the years. This meant the world to Ragan, to be able to see the doll collection together.

During one of our hospital visits, we became friends with a couple who lived in East Texas. They were there with their grandson, Austin. He had an infection that caused him to be hospitalized. Ragan found out they owned horses and told them she loved horses and was taking riding lessons. They asked if she had a horse, and she said no; before we knew it, Grandpa Rodney and Grandma Carolyn were offering Ragan one of their horses.

Once Ragan got out of the hospital, we made a trip to their home, and she was able to pick out her horse. They kept it there, but Ragan knew she could come and ride Patches any time she wanted. We made many trips through the years to ride Patches, and our friendship grew with Grandpa Rodney and Grandma Carolyn, and they soon became part of our family.

The list is endless of people who have stepped in at the right time. Although there were times we often didn't have as much as others, our "needs" were always met. You can find God in the smallest moments.

Hopeful Reflections

Reconnecting with God & Others

*"No one will be able to stand up against you all
the days of your life. As I was with Moses,
so I will be with you; I will never leave you nor forsake
you ... Have I not commanded you? Be strong and
courageous. Do not be terrified; do not be discouraged, for
the LORD your God will be with you wherever you go."*
JOSHUA 1:5, 9

I love these two scriptures listed above. With everything our family has gone through with Ragan, whenever I felt disconnected from God or others, I have leaned on those verses often throughout the years.

For many of you, I know you may be experiencing some uneasy anticipation as you bide your time until your child's upcoming doctor's appointment. Others may be waiting on results of recent tests done on your child, and then there are also those of you who are anxiously waiting to see if your child is going to need yet another surgery.

It's so hard to reach out and connect with others during this time. However, this is the very time we need to make sure we are not withdrawing from the very thing that can bring us the hope we need—other people!

People cope with worry and anxiety in different ways, and many of those ways are not healthy for you or your family. I have struggled at times with allowing anxious thoughts to consume me, and maybe some of you are dealing with that now as well.

How many of you repeatedly reenact scenes in your mind regarding situations, diagnoses, or medical issues that have not happened? We tell ourselves we are just preparing in case it ever does happen, but such thinking can consume our hearts and minds. We wrap ourselves up in a spiral of pain, grief, and bitterness over an event that hasn't even happened. When we do this to ourselves, it multiplies our suffering and causes us great physical and emotional unrest. This is not how God intended for us to live.

God has a much better solution for you and your family when you find yourself in fear of what the future might bring. In the scripture above, God is telling you that you do not have to multiply your suffering in this manner. There is a better way.

Don't disconnect. Instead, go to Him and find rest. He will strengthen you and prepare you for whatever lies ahead. He will be with you wherever you go and will transform your fear into hope, joy, confidence, and trust in Him.

Take Action:

Often when we go through difficult times, our first natural response as humans is to withdraw and disconnect. Let this be a red flag and a warning in your life to take steps to stay connected to others. Pray, go to church, find a small group, connect with a charity or a non-profit specifically created to help you through difficult times, ask for prayer, and talk. Tell your friends, co-workers, and neighbors what you are going through.

We are all like embers in a fire. When we are part of a community, we burn brighter. However, when we drift away, we begin to feel isolated and alone, and soon, our spark goes out. Don't let your spark go out. Stay connected to your community of support.

Prayer:

Dear Lord, sometimes I have withdrawn from You and others without even realizing it, wondering why I feel so isolated and alone. Help me to notice this withdrawal sooner so I can take steps to reconnect with You and others, regardless of how I feel. Help me to understand that I am never alone. In Jesus's name I pray, Amen.

Your Reflections

_____

_____

_____

_____

_____

_____

_____

_____

_____

_____

_____

_____

_____

_____

_____

_____

_____

_____

_____

_____

_____

Chapter 10

Turning Point

Overcoming Obstacles

Seasons ebb and flow, and some years are harder than others.

The year 1995 was a very hard year for Ragan. For several months, she was in and out of the hospital with the doctors trying to determine what the issue was. Finally, doctors diagnosed her problem as stemming from a hole in her intestines that was causing a major infection. They decided Ragan would have to have yet another surgery. This is never good news, and every single time, I felt her pain as if it were my own.

It started out like any other surgery. During the early morning preparations, we consoled her through her efforts to understand why she had to be going through all this again. Our family walked with her to the double doors and we said our goodbyes and promised she would see us in a few hours in the recovery room.

Although Ragan was only seven years of age, she knew the routine. As always, I watched her being wheeled past the double doors until she could no longer see me, and then I allowed myself to shed the tears I had worked so hard to hold back while in her presence. I stepped away from everyone else as well so no one would see me cry. I always felt I had to be strong...for everyone.

The family resumed their normal routines and sat in the waiting room, eager for the nurse to call and give us updates. Between updates, several family members went to the cafeteria, and we all participated in the usual small talk that takes place while anxiously waiting for the surgery to be over.

After ten hours of surgery, we finally got to see her in recovery. Ragan was still sleeping from the anesthesia but it was comforting for us to see her for a brief time. Shortly after our time there, they took her back to her hospital room. It was New Year's Eve; the hospital was quiet, and Brenda stayed with me to bring in the New Year. We laughed and giggled and celebrated with crackers and a soft drink while Ragan slept peacefully.

Early the next morning, I called the nurse in and told her Ragan wasn't acting right. She assured me it was just from having surgery the day before. We were on a different hospital floor than where we usually were, and I didn't know the staff here; nor were they familiar with us.

I explained to the nurse how many times Ragan had had surgery and I knew something was wrong. Typically, Ragan would be alert by this time after her surgeries, but she continued to be nonresponsive and began to run a fever. Throughout the day, Ragan's condition continued to worsen. That afternoon, I noticed what appeared to be bruising on her side.

I called the nurse in, and she said they would keep an eye on it. About an hour later, the bruising had moved, settling in the area she would be lying on for a period of time. The nurse then called the surgeons.

Before we knew it, Kirk and I found ourselves talking to several doctors. They all agreed that Ragan was bleeding internally. The problem was that two doctors wanted to go back in and open her up, and we did not think she would make it through the surgery. The doctor who had been with us from the first day of birth, was saying not to go back in. I remember seeing him walk down the hall to be by himself, praying before coming back to talk with Kirk and me. After listening to the options, Kirk and I decided not to have her go through another surgery.

They then moved her into the Intensive Care Unit. During the next hours, Ragan continued to grow even worse. It seemed that each hour, another machine was being brought in to monitor something.

We each sat by her bedside in the unit, finding ourselves constantly glancing at the clock and trying to let everyone have a chance to be with her. With the sound of the respirator breathing for her, and the heart monitor alarms beeping, I sat beside her for what seemed like an eternity. I tried to find a place to hold onto her body where no medical device was inserted.

Over the next couple of days, the nursing staff from the other floors who knew Ragan from her prior visits began coming to the ICU to see her. I sensed that something more was wrong and that they had seen this happen before and knew what was to follow.

During this time of being in the ICU with Ragan, I was handed this scripture/prayer. To this day, years later, I still carry it in my purse and often pray this not only for others but also for myself.

> *Find rest, Delena, in God alone; your hope*
> *comes from Him. He alone is your rock and*
> *your salvation; He is your fortress. Delena will not be*
> *shaken. Your salvation and your honor depend on God; He*
> *is your mighty rock, your refuge. Trust in Him at all times,*
> *Delena; pour out your heart to Him for God is your refuge.*
> *(This is from Psalm 62:5-8)*

Within a matter of days, her lungs began to fill with fluid. The doctors were doing everything they could to save her, but Ragan was slipping away. Looking back, it was the closest we had come to losing her since she had been born.

We were told by the doctors to say our goodbyes, because they did not foresee her surviving through the next few hours. Although I wanted peace for Ragan, I did not want to lose my "baby girl." As I sat beside her bed, I prayed, "God, please don't take my baby girl."

I walked out of her room into the waiting room to tell family members that soon Ragan would be passing away. I saw the looks that were so familiar to me from when she was first born. The waiting room was silent. The chaplain had been called to visit with us; he stayed in the waiting area saying nothing…he was simply there in case someone wanted to talk. It was an emotional time, and those who did share a few words were trying to say the right things.

Someone said something to me that had been said over and over throughout our seven years with Ragan. "God gives special-needs children to people who are strong. You are a strong person, Delena, because God won't give you more than you can handle."

I walked away from those in the waiting area and found a spot where I could be alone. I continued to pray to God, asking Him to allow Ragan more time with me. Through the years, I had begun to believe the statement about being strong because I thought I was strong. After all, that is what I had been told time and time again.

As I look back, I found myself wanting to be recognized as being strong and being able to handle it all. But while sitting in the intensive care waiting room, I was brought to my knees and I heard God's voice. *"I didn't give you Ragan because you were strong but to make you strong. Now, no matter what the outcome of this situation is, what are you going to do to glorify Me?"*

I had to understand that the statement I had been told for so long—"God never gives you more than you can handle"—was not true. God *does* give you more than you can handle, or you would never learn to turn to Him, to trust Him, and to rely on Him. If we could handle everything ourselves, then why would we need an all-powerful God?

This was a turning point in my life. Although I had started leaning back on God over the past couple of years, this is when I began to turn everything over to God, totally surrendering and relying on His strength.

Over the next few weeks, Ragan began to make progress. Each day brought its obstacles that Ragan had to overcome, but after more than a month in the Intensive Care Unit, she was able to go to a regular room. There she stayed for an additional month and finally was able to come home.

Once at home, Ragan began to share with me what she remembered experiencing while she was unconscious in the ICU. I soon realized she was speaking about what we thought were her last moments on earth with us.

She began to articulate an out-of-body experience that a seven-year-old could not describe had she not experienced this near-death occurrence herself.

She shared her memory of being above her bed, looking down on us. She could see her body in the bed while Kirk and I held on to her hands. She saw that I was crying. A warmth came over her and she saw a bright light. She felt as though she were being pulled in two directions but she soon felt herself coming back to us, and then she was lying in the bed again.

What I found so amazing about this conversation was that she was very matter of fact about it…as though it was a normal occurrence. But as a seven-year-old, she wouldn't know that it wasn't. I was very deliberate about not putting words in her mouth and just letting her share the experience. This is now a part of her testimony, and she knows that God isn't finished with her yet.

Hopeful Reflections

Overcoming Obstacles

At every point in life, there will be obstacles, and when we can recognize those obstacles, we need to understand that they are opportunities for God to show us His strength, His wisdom, and His grace.

Obstacles are a way to direct us, guide us, grow us, stretch us, and allow us to trust in His power as He works through us to show His glory to others through our circumstances.

As you allow yourself to be stretched, it is good to remember you are not alone. God is right there with you, and He will give you what you need at just the right time to be effectively used as you become victorious over the obstacles in your way.

Sometimes, we become our own obstacles. We feel that because we don't know enough or aren't big enough, strong enough, put-together enough, or wise enough, we can't be influential in the lives of others. However, know that God can use you in any circumstance, in any way, even if you don't know what to say.

Maybe a child needs to laugh while you fumble with a child's craft or read a children's book with a funny voice. Maybe a crying boy or hurting mother just needs you to sit next to them, offering them the support they need just by your presence in the room.

A smile, a hug, laughter, and a caring heart are all universal acts and can touch someone in unfathomable ways that we may never fully understand. There are no limits when you leave yourself open to God's work and are willing to do whatever is required to overcome whatever fears you have standing in the way.

Take Action:

Are you experiencing some personal obstacles that are standing in the way of your joy, hope, and peace? If so, the answer you need is within the obstacle itself. Do you feel alone and isolated? If that is an obstacle holding you back, then identify someone in your life who is lonely and isolated and connect with him or her.

Do you feel you are not having your needs met and are overwhelmed with burdens of life? If so, find someone who has a need, whether it's groceries, a lawn in need of mowing, a broken porch light, or prayer. Fill a need in someone else's life, and you will be amazed at how your own needs are met as well.

Whatever obstacle you feel is in your way, conquer it by helping remove a similar obstacle in someone else's life. In that, you just may find your own obstacles moved.

Prayer:

Dear Jesus, I know You already have the solution to any obstacle that stands in my way of finding hope, joy, and peace in You. Please use my life and work through me to overcome the obstacles in my life so I can fully experience Your joy and peace as I put all my faith, hope, and trust in You. In Jesus's name I pray, Amen.

Your Reflections

_____

_____

_____

_____

_____

_____

_____

_____

_____

_____

_____

_____

_____

_____

_____

_____

_____

_____

_____

_____

Chapter 11

New Beginnings

Revival

I often called on my dad to give me words of encouragement. He was a strong, firm man with a gentle touch. He always displayed his love and obedience to God and he raised me to have a personal relationship with my Savior.

Oftentimes, when I was feeling alone, the vision of my dad sitting in his chair in the bedroom reading his Bible would come to mind. That would be my encouragement to pick up the Bible and search for scriptures to bring me strength, and the feeling of being alone would go away. Dad and I always had a special bond, and to have seen him have that bond with Ragan is a joy that I cannot begin to express.

His words of encouragement to Ragan and to me have lifted us up so many times when I couldn't see past the obstacle that we were experiencing. He continued to encourage us daily, even when the medical obstacles slowed down.

I remember going out with friends one night and sitting in a corner of the room and thinking, *I have so much more than they do.*

Now, that was a realization for me. You see, I thought they had it all when I left that evening to spend time with them. Money, security, friends, powerful jobs, but as I looked at them and listened, I realized that I was the one blessed. I didn't know how I was going to pay the bills that month, but I had so much more peace and assurance than they had due to my relationship with Christ.

I soon started focusing on what was needed in my life and began to reignite my relationship with Christ. I had gone to a new church but was not able to go consistently due to being at the hospital so much. As time permitted, Ragan and I began to make going to church a priority.

Although we were still not consistent in our attendance due to the numerous hospital visits, I could feel God working on me and knew that this was the church that we needed to be a part of.

With that being said, months went by, and I still was not experiencing the peace and joy that the scriptures promised. No matter what I did, nothing in my life seemed to be working. I felt like I needed change in my life, but I didn't know what that change was.

I was doing all the right things, reading scriptures, going to church, joining the various Bible studies that were offered, and surrounding myself with a social group made of Christ followers, but I found myself still searching. I didn't know what I was searching for...but I was still looking. There came a point when I cried out to God, saying, "God! What am I missing in life?" I realized that I still wanted to be in control and I wasn't being totally open to God's plan. I began to cry to Him, turning it all over, asking Him to show me the way…His way. I didn't know what He would do or when, but at that point, I knew He was going to move in my life. I was then filled instantly with peace.

God began to fill my life with love, not necessarily through people but through Him. Once I began to seek Him with all my heart, I found Him. He revealed Himself to me because I sincerely sought Him. I began to feel loved, no matter how alone I was. I began to be transformed.

What I didn't know was that He was preparing me for what was to come. I remember talking with Ragan's PaPa, Dan, about how I felt I was to do something for others. My vision was to start a foundation, and I reviewed the business plan with him. Dan has always been one with an entrepreneurial mind. He encouraged me to do what God was prompting me to and even said that one day I should write a book. Anyone who knows Dan reaps the benefit of his encouragement. He is a positive person and gives you the desire to be more and to do more. I know through the years he worried about Ragan privately, but when around others, he was always positive.

I continued to think about my encounter with God in the waiting room during Ragan's surgery when He asked me—no matter the outcome with Ragan—what was I going to do to glorify Him? I knew I was called to do something, but the timing of this dream was not right yet. There was so much that needed to be done for both Ragan and myself that I could not give the attention to others that was needed if I pursued those goals at that moment.

After making the commitment to God, it was amazing how my life began to change. Prior to Ragan's experience in the ICU, I had met a wonderful person named Randy. We had not spent much time together due to Ragan's hospitalization, but we had begun developing a friendship.

During this friendship period, Ragan had her near-death experience. I later found out that Randy was experiencing mixed emotions during that time. He wanted to come to the hospital and be with me, but because we had not taken our friendship to the next level, he did not want to interfere.

One afternoon, once Ragan was out of the ICU, Randy called and said he was in the neighborhood and wanted to drop by; I told him that would be fine. When he arrived, I asked him what he was doing "in the neighborhood." His response was, "I found out that your daughter needed blood donated in her name, so I came and donated on her behalf." I knew then that Randy was a special man whom I wanted to get to know more. It wasn't until I made the commitment to God that our relationship became more. Randy had such an impact on my life. It was clear that he was a strong Christian man who had love to give...even to a mother and child who had a lot of special needs.

From that point forward, it was as if Randy had always been in our lives. He stepped right in and started being there for both me and Ragan. Our date nights often became evenings in the hallway of the hospital. Once Ragan was asleep, we would sit outside her room eating white powder donuts and drinking Dr. Pepper. Years later, it still brings a smile to my face when I see white powdered donuts.

Over the next months, not only Randy but his girls also became a part of our lives, and it felt as though they had always been a part of us. Katherine and Jennifer were so good to Ragan and began to look after her needs and protect her from obstacles as much as they could. Katherine and Jennifer have never shown jealousy toward the time that their father spent with Ragan.

Ragan has required a lot of attention through the years of being in the hospital, and there were times when the other girls' plans had to take a backseat to Ragan, but they were understanding and supportive at all costs, even if it meant they didn't get to do what they wanted. What a blessing from God!

It became apparent that God's plan was for Randy and me to blend our families in the future. We began preparing to follow God's direction and get married.

Not only did Randy and his girls accept Ragan and me, Randy's family members did as well. The Stuart family accepted us into their family, and Ragan became one of the grandchildren, with them showing no difference between her and the others. They have been so supportive throughout the years with Ragan's medical needs, and we have been blessed to have them as part of our family.

Hopeful Reflections

Transform Despair into HOPE

We see a lot of different transformations throughout our lives. Our environment and surroundings are constantly changing, and before we know it, serene landscapes have disappeared to make room for commerce, shopping malls, and condos.

We also see cuddly infants who seem to suddenly transform into moody teenagers, then transform yet again into mirrors of their parents. I think the most iconic of all are the butterflies that experience their metamorphosis inside the cocoons of caterpillars, from which they emerge biologically and beautifully transformed.

As radical as some of these transformations are, there was an even more amazing change that took place on a mountain long ago in front of Jesus's disciples Peter, James, and John:

> *"After six days Jesus took Peter, James and John with him and led them up a high mountain, where they were all alone. There he was transfigured before them. His clothes became dazzling white, whiter than anyone in the world could bleach them. And there appeared before them Elijah and Moses, who were talking with Jesus. Peter said to Jesus, 'Rabbi, it is good for us to be here. Let us put up three shelters—one for you, one for Moses and one for Elijah.' (He did not know what to say, they were so frightened.) Then a*

cloud appeared and covered them, and a voice came from the cloud: 'This is my Son, whom I love. Listen to him!' Suddenly, when they looked around, they no longer saw anyone with them except Jesus."

MARK 9:2-9

How amazing that must have been! Have you ever experienced or imagined a transformation like that? Jesus went from the visual form of a normal human being to something so glorious and luminous that the human eye could barely look upon it—it was like looking at the sun. This was a change like no one had ever seen or would see again.

As miraculous as that change seems, did you know the same thing can happen to us? Romans 12:2 tells us, *"Do not conform any longer to the pattern of this world, but be transformed by the renewing of your mind. Then you will be able to test and approve what God's will is – his good, pleasing and perfect will."*

For many of us, we know we are a part of the family of God, but we don't feel we've changed much; we haven't experienced a transformation like the one described above. So, what do we do?

This transformation won't happen without effort on our part. To be transformed, we have to renew—change and add new data, experiences, and behaviors—our minds. We do this by spending more time with God, reading His Word, the Bible, and communicating with Him through prayer. The more time we spend with Him, the more we become like Him. When we change, this change spreads through us and out into the world around us, making all things new, different, and transformed.

The world around us needs hope, but it can't acquire that hope on its own. In the midst of their sadness, people need your help, your light, and your transformation to bring them that hope. However, they won't be able to recognize your ability to help if you look and act just like one of them. People need to see the difference in you so they too can have the hope of being different as well.

Take Action:

As you spend time with God today, ask Him to transform you so you can bring more hope and joy to the world, so that you too can display a heart that is luminous, "dazzling white, whiter than anyone in the world could bleach."

Prayer:

Dear Lord, please turn my despair into hope and joy in You alone so my heart can shine and reflect Your glory. In Jesus's name I pray, Amen.

Your Reflections

_____

_____

_____

_____

_____

_____

_____

_____

_____

_____

_____

_____

_____

_____

_____

_____

_____

_____

_____

Chapter 12

Bearing Fruit

Shared Experiences

Throughout the next few years, Ragan battled with an issue for which her doctors could not figure out the cause. We were basically told to settle with the conclusion that this issue may not resolve itself. At that point, as her mother, I was not going to give up. I knew something wasn't right and needed to get to the bottom of it. After overcoming some hurdles with insurance, I was able to have her seen by another urologist. Through his determination to discover the reason for Ragan's discomfort, he found that Ragan needed another surgery. We had known she would need this surgery when she got older, but because of the problems she was experiencing, we decided to plan for this procedure earlier than expected.

Once again, Ragan amazed me with her willingness to go through another trip to the hospital. Ragan underwent this surgery and recovered well. She had been in a lot of pain during this time but always had her chin up and continued to get stronger. Naturally we were now hesitant about any surgery.

On the day of the surgery, our families experienced the power of God. There were four doctors scheduled to do this surgery, most of whom we had met at some point during Ragan's other procedures. However, within the first hour of the surgery, one of the doctors came from the operating room to advise us not to continue and to wait for Ragan to get older. This particular doctor was a new doctor to our family, and she was not familiar with everything we had already been through. Nor was this doctor familiar with how well I knew the needs of my child.

As the doctor explained her point of view as to why to wait to complete the surgery, I felt the eyes of every family member looking at me...waiting for a decision. No one wanted to speak up or say anything.

I sat there trying to process what the doctor was saying, and as society dictates, I believed we are supposed to take a doctor's advice. After all, he or she is the doctor. Finally, succumbing to the pressure, I told her I would go along with her advice to discontinue the surgery. She quickly departed to tell the other surgeons who were in the operating room that the decision had been made to postpone the surgery.

However, as she walked away, I felt as though I had made a tremendous mistake. I knew in my heart Ragan was ready for this day, and I did not know how to make the new doctor understand the process we had gone through to initially make this decision. All I could do at that point was pray and ask God for help.

As I sat there in silent prayer, everyone around me was so quiet and still that you could have heard a pin drop. No one was saying a word.

Within minutes, the other three doctors came charging into the waiting room, and they asked for Kirk and me to speak with them in the conference room. There the plastic surgeon advised us that he could make this operation a success. The other two doctors agreed with him. As I looked around the room at the doctors, I knew my prayers were being answered. God had made it possible for the decision to be changed in order for the surgery to continue. God is an awesome God, and because of His will, the surgery was a success! This surgery lasted twelve and half hours, but because of what I had seen God do, it was used to glorify Him.

I not only experienced this special time as a God-moment in my life, but it was also a wonderful testimony for our family members and friends. I believe that Ragan and all our family members are here to be a witness to others and to tell the world about all the miracles great and small God performs in our lives every day.

Just three months after her surgery, Ragan was back riding horses. While watching her and her cousin Rebecca, I realized how wonderful it was to see her enjoyment of life. She takes nothing for granted. She loves spending time with her family and enjoying each day to the fullest.

One time during one of our many talks, Ragan asked me if I knew that when you get to heaven, you got a new body with no scars or problems. She said she could not wait to get there and have God give her a new body. The difference in the two of us was that my heart broke during our conversation, wanting her to have a healthy body here on earth, but Ragan was so sincere and positive and knew God would take care of her; and her excitement for that day to come was unbelievable.

Ragan completed two more major spinal surgeries at the end of the following year. We were told the recovery time would be at least a year of no activities. Basically, she would only be able to walk, stand, or sit for any length of time. Once again, Ragan proved them wrong.

Through all of this, Ragan's sense of humor never left. Because at birth she had no skin covering her abdominal area, she was not born with a belly button. She always wanted a belly button, and before going into surgery, she wrote a note to the doctor to remind him to make one. She held onto it until she got into the surgery room and then showed it to him prior to falling asleep. She asked for him to pierce it while he was in there.

Needless to say, the doctor followed her orders in making the belly button but didn't pierce it. Later, I found out that her granddad had promised to provide the naval ring if it was going to be pierced. The love that a grandchild can give still amazes me as well as how grandparents truly change over the years in their rules—my dad would never have provided a navel ring for me!

During the years, God has shown me His love and grace. I was able to start a ministry at church that assists families while their children are in the hospital. My goal was to be there for them through their struggles and show them what an awesome God we have and that it is so important to turn to Him and not try to do everything ourselves.

I have been fortunate to have my family and friends there for support, but one person continued to be in my life during so many doctor visits, trips to the hospital, and the daily ups and downs.

Although her son and I divorced, my mother-in-law Brenda showed me so much support, and even today I can call on her any time for comfort or help. It is my desire to model that in order to help others who are less fortunate.

Hopeful Reflections

Importance of Fruit Bearing

"My command is this: Love each other as I have loved you. Greater love has no one than this, that he lay down his life for his friends. You are my friends if you do what I command. I no longer call you servants, because a servant does not know his master's business. Instead, I have called you friends, for everything that I learned from my Father I have made known to you. You did not choose me, but I chose you and appointed you to go and bear fruit–fruit that will last. Then the Father will give you whatever you ask in my name. This is my command: Love each other."

JOHN 15:12-17

Anyone who has tended any type of plant, garden, vineyard, orchard, or crop can attest to the importance of cultivating the soil and intentionally nurturing delicate vegetation throughout every stage of growth. It's not always easy, and sometimes sacrifices have to be made as we leave the comfort and warmth of our homes to go out and pull weeds, implement pest control, water, trim, and harvest, as well as sometimes covering our plants to protect them from whatever weather or storms are at hand. However, we persevere because of the light of hope that one day, we will see the results of our labor.

It is no accident that seeds, planting crops, and managing vineyards was the subject matter for many of the parables—or stories—Jesus used in His teachings. The love and care it takes to raise up a good crop is similar to the effort we need to give to our day-to-day relationships. In John 15:12, Jesus said, *"My command is this: Love each other as I have loved you."*

The next verse tells us that the greatest expression of our love is to give one's life for one's friends. Jesus did more than teach this principle; He actually lived it out. That's exactly what Jesus did for us. We may never be asked to die for our loved ones, but are we at least showing them the same type of love through the way we nurture and care for them?

So, I have to ask myself, "Do I extend my love and care for others beyond the borders of my own garden? Does what I do measure up to the example Jesus gave us in Scripture?"

In verses 13-16, we are given five principles we can follow to show genuine love to those who are both intimately involved in our lives and those who only cross our path but for a moment:

1) Genuine love is sacrificial. A sacrifice is the act of giving up something precious for the good of another.

2) Genuine love is demonstrated through willing obedience and is the expression of a willing heart, not a begrudging heart.

3) Genuine love always communicates the truth. Sometimes we must be very careful in doing this because truth can be painful.

4) Genuine love will cause us to take the initiative in meeting the legitimate needs of others.

5) Genuine love will always bear fruit with abiding results.

As followers of Jesus Christ and His teachings, our goal should be to produce fruit that is both abundant and enduring. In order for us to accomplish that task, we need to be diligent to ensure we produce quantity (an abundance), and we need patience to ensure quality so that our fruit endures to make an impact on those we are serving.

Both virtues working together (diligence and patience) are of utmost importance. Being active without diligence and results is just busy-work; busyness does many things but nothing well, and patience unaccompanied by diligence easily degenerates into laziness.

Bearing fruit is in our honorable nature as living beings, but it has even more importance as we come to understand why we need to follow this call. First, as we bear fruit, we are passing forward our faith into the lives of those we are serving. This is one way we show gratitude to God for all He has done. Producing fruit is also where we find true joy and fulfillment. Jesus even says that His joy will remain in us and our joy will be full!

In verse 17, Jesus reiterated His command that we love one another. Love is the great motivator in the Christian life. I pray that you will nurture and cultivate your love for others and allow it to mature as you grow in your relationship with Jesus Christ. Our hope is that you produce abundant and lasting fruit that will impact not only your family today but also the generations to come!

Take Action:

Write down different things you can do throughout your day to channel God's love and power to others, which is a form of bearing fruit—anything from your attitude as you drive to smiling and greeting those in your path.

Keeping an outward focus on God, His love, and His desire to spread peace, hope, and love is an important step when desiring to bear fruit and nourish others with God's power working through you.

Remember to allow God to use you His way, which could be worlds apart from how you thought you would be utilized in this life. Stay open to His still, small voice.

Pray and ask God to help you recognize those opportunities where you can step up and be used to bear fruit and channel His love to someone else today.

Prayer:

Dear Lord, I know we are supposed to be used for Your glory, but sometimes, I think I am so busy taking care of myself that I miss Your still, small voice. Thank you for wanting to work through me to touch the lives of others and please help me to seize those opportunities that You bring my way. In Jesus's name I pray, Amen.

Your Reflections

_____

_____

_____

_____

_____

_____

_____

_____

_____

_____

_____

_____

_____

_____

_____

_____

_____

_____

_____

_____

Chapter 13

Being an Advocate

Defender for Others

Whatever you've been through may have been preparing you for a great mission or ministry. Pain isn't a requirement for doing God's work but it's often a part of the burden we must carry as believers who lay down their life for Christ.

Although mentally Ragan excelled with no problem, she continued to struggle in everyday physical accomplishments. Unable to do many things, Ragan still took part in activities with her friends. I saw the pain in her eyes when all the children could ride a bike without training wheels or skate for any distance and she was left on the sidelines, watching them do what she so desperately wanted to do as well.

However, she did not stay on the sidelines for long. Her fiery determination brought her to accomplishments that she didn't even know she could achieve, and the family supported her in her desires and ambitions. Randy and the girls began to take her to the church parking lot on Saturdays and spent most of the day teaching Ragan how to ride a bike and letting her practice. Soon, by the age of eight, she was able to ride her bike without training wheels!

Many of the students at her school were also inquisitive but understanding. "What happened to you?" they asked. "Have you always been sick?"

Even at such a young age, they soon came to admire her independence and outlook on life. Children with chronic illnesses often begin to feel isolated since they cannot physically see anyone else quite like them, so they withdraw and disconnect from their peers.

However, Ragan had a special friend, Brandy, who through grade school saw to it that Ragan didn't fall into that isolation trap. When Ragan would be in the hospital, Brandy would be right there with her. Brandy's parents were so supportive of the friendship and would not think twice of bringing Brandy to the hospital in order to have sleepovers in the hospital room. Brandy kept Ragan informed of what was going on at school and was a very good friend to her, accepting her just the way she was.

Ragan's being mature socially was often misleading when it came to her level of education. We began to see she was not able to complete the work that other second and third graders were doing.

A teacher recognized this as well and began to process Ragan into the special needs program, which would allow her to be coded as "other health impaired (code 504)" in order to get additional assistance. Unfortunately, the district did not agree with this, which started an ongoing battle as I became Ragan's advocate for appropriate education. I realized that if I did not go to battle for her, no one else would.

Although the school district performed testing, they determined she was delayed due to missing so much school. I did not find comfort in that since I could see her struggles.

I had her endure several tests from outside educational experts, which showed her IQ to be above average. Based on this and other findings, it was determined some of her struggles had not been due to missing school but because she had a learning disorder—dyslexia. Sadly, the school district would not recognize our results, nor would they provide any dyslexia tutoring.

During this time, I did go before the Educational Board of Texas for a hearing with the intent of getting additional assistance for Ragan with her studies. I was told by the state judge that as long as she made a 70, they were not required to provide further assistance.

This did not settle with me, so I was told that I could file a formal case with the court system, but this would take money and time with no guarantees. Much of this happened prior to marrying Randy, so I was a single mom and needed to work full time while also being available to stay at the hospital with my child during her surgeries and illnesses. That kind of schedule left me with no ability to pursue the case.

This was a period of time that, once again, I felt so isolated and alone. I often found myself asking "Where are you, God? Why can't Ragan just live a normal life and get what she deserves with her education?"

I saw such a smart little girl not being given the opportunity to excel, and due to the lack of money and time, I couldn't do anything about it—legally.

Instead of spending the funds to go to court, I decided to use that money to assist Ragan, so I secured a personal tutor for her. She received tutoring for her learning disorders for several years independent of the school district and began making the A-B honor roll shortly after the extra assistance began.

For a couple of school years, Ragan went to school for half days and was taught at home in the afternoons. This was due to her strength decreasing and because she had now been diagnosed with chronic intestinal pseudo-obstruction. This is an illness that causes severe stomach pains, similar to migraine headaches, but in the abdominal area. Our fight with the district continued through these years. It seemed as though they were against giving Ragan any additional assistance, regardless of the circumstances.

Because of all the obstacles we faced, Ragan's school situation was a priority in our prayers.

When Ragan started middle school, she decided to try attending for the full day. Although I was excited about Ragan wanting to go to school full time, I dreaded the fight I knew I would face with the district.

We had had several obstacles in previous years with the district, and I didn't know if I had it in me to fight for Ragan's needs again. However, as usual, God showed us that if we are patient and wait on Him, He will supply us with an answer.

This was quite an adjustment, but through this transition, God placed a principal at Ragan's school who was a

Christian, and I could tell he truly wanted to help meet her needs. Although there was a learning curve for the staff, his desire was reflected through them, and each member wanted to do what was best for Ragan.

As I dropped her off the first day of middle school, I couldn't help but shed a few tears. Unlike most moms, I wasn't shedding tears that my baby girl was growing up… my tears were thanking God that I got to experience this special day—her first full day of school—and that she had survived this long to attend middle school.

When she was born, I honestly didn't know if she would live long enough for me to share these important, special days. Ragan has shown me such joy, and I have learned through small experiences such as this that each moment and experience is unique and special; none of us should take any of them for granted.

Socially, Ragan has always been mature beyond her years, and as Ragan started getting older, this caused her some isolation through her pre-teen years with others her own age. While other girls were fighting over popularity and status with boys, Ragan was fighting for her survival as she continued to suffer from multiple illnesses. Thankfully, though, through the years, she began to gravitate to more mature individuals who were more focused on issues that truly mattered.

Shortly after starting middle school, it was time for her to be re-evaluated by the district in order to remain coded, which is done through an Admission, Review and Dismissal (ARD) meeting. We had had these meetings several times each year since second grade and quite honestly, I went into the meeting thinking this would be yet another waste of time. But this meeting confirmed that Ragan's test results revealed she did have a learning disorder. The staff could not believe that she had not been coded with such a disorder through the district prior to that date. This was the next step in obtaining needed evaluations to give Ragan the assistance that she needed so she could complete the rest of her schooling with as few obstacles as possible.

I remember asking the staff to repeat their findings of the test. I looked over at Randy with amazement. Ragan would finally get the help she needed through the district.

Hopeful Reflections

Defender for Others

"Speak up for those who cannot speak for themselves, for the rights of all who are destitute. Speak up and judge fairly; defend the rights of the poor and needy."
PROVERBS 31:8-9

Often during troubled times, it's hard to have the strength to stand up and speak for others. You may feel like you have enough on your plate and that the situation would be just another time-consuming issue. But, if we are focusing on being like Christ, then we do need to speak up for those who cannot speak for themselves.

When you stand up for people, you show that you're "on their side" when they need help. This builds long-term loyalty, trust, credibility, and commitment. It also shows that you are focused on others' well-being and interests, rather than on yourself.

Although, there are times when being an advocate for the one we are caring for is necessary, advocating for others truly does change your focus from the current situation you are experiencing to one where you can see progress for the other person. It turns the focus on their needs rather than your own needs.

Take Action:

Take some time to look outside of yourself and see who may need an advocate. You may be surprised that that person is right there in front of you and that it may not take much time away from your day-to-day routine. Being an advocate doesn't always mean something "life-changing" needs to take place. It could be a simple gesture in their moment of need.

Prayer:

Dear God, I come before You today, asking You to reveal someone who needs me to stand up for him or her. Although I am working through troubled times myself, I know that to grow to be more like You, I need to focus on the needs of others. I pray that through my efforts and actions, the person will see Your love. In Jesus's name, Amen.

Your Reflections

_____

_____

_____

_____

_____

_____

_____

_____

_____

_____

_____

_____

_____

_____

_____

_____

_____

_____

Chapter 14

Determination

Run the Race...Finish Strong

At the age of fourteen, Ragan visited California to pursue a dream she had for a few years in wanting to be an actor. I hadn't let her get too involved in this because of the many hospital visits she was undergoing. But by then, the surgeries had decreased, and she was able to go to school and keep her grades up. She was able to be involved in several acting productions. On our way to California for our first trip, I explained to her that people live there for years and never obtain agents. She politely told me it was a goal and that she would accomplish it. While in California, she accomplished it. She auditioned for acting agents and was able to sign on with one.

As I listened to Ragan, she explained during her interviews that she wanted to become an actor because she wanted to show others that you can accomplish anything you set your mind to. I realized how determined she is to live life to the fullest. She would achieve many goals in her life, I was confident of that.

By the age of fifteen, Ragan had completed the last of her planned surgeries. She had been to the operating room over forty times and had had multiple day procedures in addition to the surgeries. I knew there would be more to come for Ragan medically, but it was such a joy to know that the planned surgeries were over and she could now focus on the things that were important to her.

Ragan continued with her daily battles. One major problem that Ragan faced was an allergy to latex, which was life-threatening. This kept her from many activities in the daily environment. But her positive outlook continued. Due to so many allergic reactions in school, she completed her education through a home school program. She also had a wheelchair that was not used daily but used when she was going to walk for any length of time.

Her determination kept her from using it very often, but she knew her limits. She still has issues with keeping her strength up continuously, but she knows when to stop and take a break in order to get the rest her body requires. She has good days and bad when it comes to pain, but she is going to be sure that you only see her on her good days.

While acting, Ragan realized that God did not intend acting as a career for her. She enjoyed it but felt that God had other plans for her. She had an interest in fashion and wanted to pursue a career in that industry and do inspirational speaking. Her first public speaking engagement was for the staff of Zig Ziglar. Ragan always does things big, and so, it was no surprise that she was able to make this speaking engagement a success.

On the way to this engagement, I asked her what she wanted to accomplish by speaking with Zig Ziglar and his staff. Her response shouldn't have astounded me. She said that if she could reach one person in sharing God's love with him or her, then she had accomplished what she came for.

After speaking to the staff and meeting with Zig Ziglar, we were walking to the car, when a gentleman stopped us in the parking lot and asked my husband if he was a salesperson. Randy had his arms full of Zig Ziglar's tapes and books that had been given to us. Randy explained where we had just come from, and the man asked Ragan to give him a condensed version of her testimony and what she had shared with them. He listened intently. After she finished, he looked straight in her eyes and said, "I needed to hear that today."

He continued to share some things he was going through personally and Ragan was able to share God's Word and show him God's love through her words. When we got in the car, Randy looked into the back seat and told Ragan that she had reached the one person she was looking for... mission accomplished.

We couldn't wait to see what God had in store for her. She definitely had a message to share. After graduating from high school, she decided to pursue her fashion career by opening up her own boutique. It is no surprise to us that she made it happen.

She met with individual business owners to gain knowledge from them, set up her budget, and continued to set her goal of her opening date. She was also able to move into her own place after graduating. I remember leaving her apartment for the first time after getting her settled and my eyes filling up with tears once again due to the accomplishments she had made and for God's provisions. There was once a time when I didn't know if she would live to be eighteen years old, let alone live on her own.

Ragan didn't live far from us and visited often to get groceries from our refrigerator and pantry. Like any young person on a budget, she found ways for her needs to be met. As I watched her drive off in her car after visiting with me one time, I truly thanked God for what He had given us. My heart raced when I thought that years earlier, we had been told she might not make it through the first day of her life. Although Ragan does not realize the impact she has made on so many individuals, it is clear to me that God's plan has always been in place and she is honoring Him each day.

Hopeful Reflections

Finish Everything and Do It Well

"Do you not know that in a race all the runners run,
but only one receives the prize? Run in such a way as
to get the prize. Everyone who competes in the games goes
into strict training. They do it to get a crown that will
not last; but we do it to get a crown that will last forever.
Therefore I do not run like a man running aimlessly; I do
not fight like a man beating the air. No, I beat my body and
make it my slave so that after I have preached to others,
I myself will not be disqualified for the prize."
1 CORINTHIANS 9: 24-27

Have you ever wanted something so desperately that despite various hindrances and setbacks, you persevered? Although the road to the finish line can be frustrating and filled with so many ups and downs, if you keep your eyes on the prize, God will give you the strength to keep on going and to finish strong.

Jesus's whole assignment while on earth was to finish the work His Father had sent Him to do. Jesus was motivated to finish everything He did and to do it well and strong. He was able to do so by keeping His eye on the prize.

Oftentimes as we have trials, obstacles, and hardships, it causes us to want to quit. This is when it is important to keep our eyes on Jesus and know that He has gone before us to lead us on the path He has chosen for us. It might be dark and lonely, but remember you are not alone and know you can finish the race!

The apostle Paul was a tremendous visionary, full of passion. He pursued his vision, no matter the cost. I would encourage you to read more about Paul. Two-thirds of the New Testament was written by the apostle because he counted the cost and depended on the Holy Spirit for guidance and direction every step of the way.

Take Action:

Even though you may be in the midst of trials, it is important you take some time to set goals for yourself and your family. Pray for God to open your schedule to allow you to focus and to see His plans for you. Although you may not be able to accomplish everything at this very moment, God will begin to use your situation to mold you to finish strong.

Prayer:

Dear Heavenly Father, before the troubles I am experiencing, I had goals and desires for my life. I know that the focus has changed to the situation I am currently in, but I am asking You to begin to use this time to mold me. Infuse me with strength as I choose Your will. In Jesus's name, Amen.

Your Reflections

_____

_____

_____

_____

_____

_____

_____

_____

_____

_____

_____

_____

_____

_____

_____

_____

_____

_____

_____

_____

_____

_____

_____

_____

_____

_____

_____

_____

_____

_____

_____

_____

_____

_____

_____

_____

_____

_____

_____

_____

_____

_____

Chapter 15

Expectancy

Anticipation of God's Will

My life changed considerably over the next few years from having multiple doctors' visits and hospital stays for Ragan's medical issues to one of full-time church ministry.

I had resigned from the corporate world and was working in a church. My role was overseeing a ministry to families with children experiencing catastrophic medical illnesses or injuries. This in turn led to my overseeing all the care ministries. I later completed a chaplain course in order to be certified as a chaplain and also became licensed as a minister. God has shown me how He has used Ragan's situation to reach others and how it has changed my life and priorities.

I was blessed with a husband, Randy, who loved the Lord with all his heart, and with three grown daughters who were now living on their own. Our life was beginning to move into the next phase—no children at home, possible early retirement. As the life we had once known was in the midst of changing, we began to plan for our future. I was working at the church full time, and Randy was involved as a leader of the motorcycle ministry there. We were enjoying our new normal and were living life to the fullest, enjoying this next phase of life. But God's plan for me was different.

Randy and a friend decided to ride their motorcycles to our ranch in South Texas for a week. I remember telling him that I was worried about their trip. I had never been worried before, but for some reason, this time felt different. As they pulled out of our driveway, Randy promised to call me throughout the drive to assure me everything was okay. I felt completely unsettled until I had heard they'd made it safely.

Throughout the week, we spoke, and it sounded like they were having a wonderful time. By the end of the week, they were getting ready to sell some cattle, and on Friday afternoon, he called, so excited that they had made a good sale.

The weather was gorgeous, and they had decided to go take a ride on the back-country roads. I told him to enjoy the ride and to take some time to thank God for the cattle sale. That was around 2:00 p.m., when I would hear Randy's voice for the last time. Within a few hours after our call, I received a call from my brother-in-law, telling me Randy had been involved in a motorcycle accident and had not survived.

I remember being at the house by myself getting ready for a quiet evening. I had already ordered pizza and was cleaning out my closet. Funny how you remember those types of things.

As I heard the news, I fell to the floor, crying and screaming to God. Within hours, my home was full of family and friends.

This time seemed different from times in the past with Ragan when I had been surrounded by people. I was in complete peace and didn't feel the loneliness that I had felt so many times before. As I reflect back on that moment, I know the peace I felt was from God. Don't confuse the peace with me not hurting. My heart was so heavy, but the sense of loneliness wasn't there. My relationship with God being where it was at that very moment is what got me through such a difficult time.

Randy was an extraordinary man who was committed to helping Ragan in any way necessary, and he was my rock to lean on through many difficult times. Randy, Katherine, and Jennifer took Ragan and me in to be a part of their family and have shown unconditional love toward us in so many ways, for which I will always be thankful. Because of my walk with God, I was able to move forward with my life even though it looked different from what I had planned. I received comfort from God on the tough days and was able to reflect on the time I had shared with Randy.

I asked God shortly after Randy's passing to give me a word to focus on. The word was "expectancy." I have taken this word and tried to live using it in my day-to-day walk, making sure that I look at each day with faith that God will exceed my greatest desire.

Hopeful Reflections

Choosing to be Expectant

*"Now to him who is able to do immeasurably
more than all we ask or imagine, according to his
power that is at work within us."*
EPHESIANS 3:20

To have expectancy means "having or showing an excited feeling that something is about to happen." Often, we find ourselves going through the motions because we are involved in so much and we miss "the moment."

Expectation produces faith. What if we approached whatever we do with expectancy, believing that "something is about to happen," such as a marriage being restored, a sickness being healed, or a lost life being saved?

Whatever you're walking through today or whatever season you might find yourself in, I want to encourage you that we have a choice to be expectant. We get to stand on the truth that God is who He says He is and He will do what He says He will do.

Take Action:

Wake up each morning and ask God to give you the faith you need to expect His mighty power to work in you. Throughout the day, seek Him and be excited for what is going to come. As you begin to pursue Him in all you do, you will be able to see what He is doing, even in the difficult times.

Prayer:

Dear Heavenly Father, I come to You today, asking You to give me faith to rely on You. I want to be expectant of Your work and what You have planned for me today. I thank You in advance for the things to come. In Jesus's name, Amen.

Your Reflections

_____

_____

_____

_____

_____

_____

_____

_____

_____

_____

_____

_____

_____

_____

_____

_____

_____

_____

_____

Closing Words

Over the next few years, I began to focus on my work in helping others through the ministry. I knew that it was a matter of time before God would open the door for me to begin a foundation to support families that have children with medical issues. God had used my time at the church to help me gain knowledge as to how to structure such a nonprofit.

As I began to seek God in my next stage of life, God granted me love again, bringing Dan into my life. We truly enjoy our time together. As we developed a relationship, we soon decided to marry. He supported me in leaving my church position to begin the nonprofit.

He became not only a supporter but holds a leadership position within the foundation. Ragan's HOPE is a nonprofit that assists families with children who have medical issues. It truly is a blessing to share this cause with Dan. I am amazed at the sensitivity he shows to me, even though he did not experience the years of raising Ragan, and his understanding that Randy is still very much a part of our lives. He is a man of God who ensures that Christ is over our relationship and at the center of all we do.

I decided to begin writing this book within weeks of a family celebration...Ragan's wedding. It seemed the right time to begin this project as we praise what He has done in her life. God had brought her a very special man, Jason, and a son, Ethan. This was truly a celebration honoring God for giving us Ragan, for a full life, and now for her to start her own family. As she walked down the sandy beach aisle, barefoot, with flowers in her hair, my eyes filled with tears, and my heart pounded like it did while I was in the elevator on my way to see her in the ICU for the first time. All through the ceremony, images flashed through my mind from her childhood on up to this very moment. What a gift I have been given.

Through the years, I was faithful in praying for that special someone for Ragan. Although we did not know what the future held for her as far as whether she would live independently or what her life expectancy would be, as her mother, I was committed to pray for this union.

Shortly after Jason and Ragan's wedding, they began the process of Ragan formally adopting Ethan. I am in awe of the commitment that she showed in becoming his mother. He became her world the minute they met, and she has given everything to meet his needs. Ethan is a joy to us all, and I say that God has a sense of humor because Ethan is so much like Ragan—full of life with lots of questions! I absolutely love being "Oma."

Once again, God is good! As a child, we always told Ragan that some mommies carry a child in their tummies and others adopt. With the medical issues Ragan has experienced, she is not able to have children, but God made sure that she is experiencing motherhood by bringing Ethan into her life.

It has taken me a few years to complete this book. Life seemed to have gotten in the way. But now that I have completed it, I am reminded that our story will continue, not knowing what the future holds but confident that God is in control. I hope this book has brought you encouragement. As I stated in the introduction, I am praying for those who read it and hope that you feel God's presence and comfort in His words on these pages.

Although Ragan still has tough days, she continues to focus on her family. These past few years, she has developed some more health complications but endures them with grace. What did this adversity teach us? To have faith and be patient. God has a plan.

I am truly grateful for having not only an extraordinary daughter but also a wonderful young woman whom I consider my best friend and who has a love for God that is immeasurable. Her strength and determination still amaze me daily. God has given her such a heart that bears so much fruit as she daily lives out her desires to help others, instead of dwelling on her own problems. This truly makes her a remarkable person, and I am honored that God chose me to be her mother.

A Note from Ragan

Finding HOPE During Uncertainty: A Story I Thought I knew...

Dear Reader,

This book you hold in your hands is not just my story.

In reality the "story" I thought I knew was so much more. My hero, my best friend, the woman I look up to the most, my Momma, has captured my soul deeper than ever before. (Trust me, she will steal yours as well.)

Reading these pages, a story I personally lived, I'm left with new insight. Not because I didn't already know the outcome, but because for the first time I have slowly started to see and embrace the struggles my family faced, to truly understand what it meant for them to fear the unknown.

Everyone's story is different, even when they are living in the *same* story. We all bear forms of tragedy and suffering. We can all make the choice to focus on tragedy and inadequacies. As you read *Finding HOPE During Uncertainty,* may you be touched by my Momma's heartfelt words of wisdom. Her words come from a place of vulnerability, a place of pure honesty. I hope you choose to find grace for yourself and others, paired with an unfathomable amount of gratitude, with greater HOPE, and a desire to embrace all that has been divinely orchestrated in your life.

"Gratitude bestows reverence, allowing us to encounter everyday epiphanies, those transcendent moments of 'AWE' that change forever how we experience life and the world."
~JOHN MILTON, POET

My Mother,

I look at you and often wonder how I got so fortunate to be given the greatest gift of being your daughter. Until I became a mother, I never fully understood the love of a parent. Reading your story left me speechless and in total awe of you. When I came into the world, you didn't see a "broken" baby. In your eyes I was a beautiful angel.

I am so fortunate to have you as my role model, my best friend, and greatest cheerleader.

You are a humble Godly woman, and you inspire me daily just by living your life. Your guidance when I feel completely lost or uncertain never fails to be just the words and encouragement I need to tackle whatever is before me.

As a child I may have not always loved the "suck it up buttercup" mantra you laid out for me. But looking back now I see that you were not pushing me past my boundaries. You were holding me up, showing me the strength I had inside. You gave me the reassurance to live my life to the fullest. You truly are one of a kind.

Over the years I have always known that if I can be half the woman you are, I will be completely happy, I will have succeeded. You are all that I strive to be. You are my Hero!

I love you!

Forever your Baby Girl,
Ragan Danielle

About the Author

Delena Stuart-Watson's debut book, *Finding HOPE During Uncertainty,* was written to encourage others as they go through difficult times. Delena knew years ago that a book was in the making but waited for God's timing for it to be written. Her inspiration comes from her own story and experiences which she hopes will inspire others to not only endure but embrace what they are going through.

Delena is married and has three grown daughters. She and her husband, Dan, enjoy spending time with family, especially with their grandson Ethan. They enjoy traveling and visiting unique towns, beaches, and independently owned restaurants.

In addition to holding a leadership position in the corporate sector, Delena is also the founder of a non-profit organization, a minister, and a public speaker. She has received several awards in each of these professional disciplines.

Through her national non-profit, Ragan's HOPE (a volunteer-driven foundation), she and her team help families nationally, as well as globally, not only to endure but to embrace their future.

Delena's passion is to serve others who have children with medical issues and to share her story of living at a hospital over the years with her daughter Ragan.

Delena enjoys speaking to audiences with various interests. Her speaking topics include leadership, patient advocacy, navigating the health-care industry, overcoming adversity, and the power of faith.

To learn more about Ragan's HOPE, please visit **www.raganshope.org.**

To schedule Delena for a speaking engagement, please visit **www.embracingstrengths.com.**